<u>Osoby:</u>

VYSLANEC
1. KRÁL
2. POLICAJT
3. MINISTR
4. ČARODĚJ
5. SELKA
6. HONZA
7. DĚDEK
8. ŽID
9. MANIČKA
10. JENÍČEK
SMRT.

<u>SCÉNY:</u>

ULICE
KRÁL. SÍŇ
KOMN. ČARODĚJE
CIRKUS.

<u>Regisity:</u>

Mikrofon
Trůn
Zvonek.

The Jewish Publication Society
Philadelphia and Jerusalem 5755/1995

The English-language edition is
distributed by
The Jewish Publication Society
1930 Chestnut Street
Philadelphia, PA 19103
U.S.A.

Library of Congress Cataloging-in-Publication Data

Je mojí vlastí hradba ghett? English.

We are children just the same: *Vedem*, the secret magazine by the boys of Terezín / prepared and selected from the magazine *Vedem (In the Lead)* by Marie Rút Křížková, Kurt Jiří Kotouč, and Zdeněk Ornest; translated from the Czech by R. Elizabeth Novak; edited by Paul R. Wilson; with a foreword by Václav Havel.

p. cm.

ISBN 0-8276-0534-X

1. Terezín (Czech Republic: Concentration camp). 2. Holocaust, Jewish (1939–1945)–Czechoslovakia–Personal narratives. 3. Czechoslovakia–Ethnic relations. 4. Terezín (Czech Republic: Concentration camp)–Literary collections. 5. Holocaust, Jewish (1939–1945)–Literary collections. 6. Children's writings, Czech–Translations into English. 7. Holocaust, Jewish (1939–1945), in art. 8. Children's art–Czechoslovakia. I. Křížková, Marie Rút. II. Kotouč, Kurt Jiří. III. Ornest, Zdeněk. IV. Novak, R. Elizabeth. V. Wilson, Paul (Paul R.). VI. *Vedem*. VII. Title.

D805.C9J413 1994

940.53'18–dc20   94–12698

CIP

Kurt Korálek
(b. 1932, perished)
"Fire"
Aquarelle, 295 × 220 mm
Jewish Museum, Prague, Inv. No. 129485

WE ARE CHILDREN
JUST THE SAME

Vedem, the Secret Magazine

by the Boys of Terezín

WE ARE CHILDREN
JUST THE SAME
Vedem, the Secret Magazine
by the Boys of Terezín

Prepared and selected from
Vedem (In the Lead)
by Marie Rút Křížková, Kurt Jiří Kotouč,
and Zdeněk Ornest

With commemorative texts by
Věra Sommerová, Ota Ginz, Miriam Ginzová,
and Eva Ginzová-Pressburgerová
Foreword by Václav Havel
Translation from the Czech by R. Elizabeth Novak
Edited by Paul R. Wilson
Documentary photographs supplied by
the Archives of the Jewish Museum, Prague,
the Memorial of Terezín,
and the Museum of Czech Literature, Prague
Original photography by Vlasta Gronská
Typographic design and layout by Jaroslav Sůra
Frontispiece: Yard in Terezín. Watercolor
by Pavel Sonnenschein.

Jacket design and art by Nachman Elsner
Copyright © 1995 by Aventinum, Prague
English-language edition copyright
© 1995 by The Jewish Publication Society,
Philadelphia and Jerusalem
Printed in Slovakia
2/98/03/51-01

Unknown artist
"View of a Small yard in Terezín"
Aquarelle, 105 × 150 mm
Jewish Museum, Prague, Inv. No. 129184

Terezín – an aerial view
from the Small Fortress.
Jewish Museum, Prague,
Neg. No. 30039.

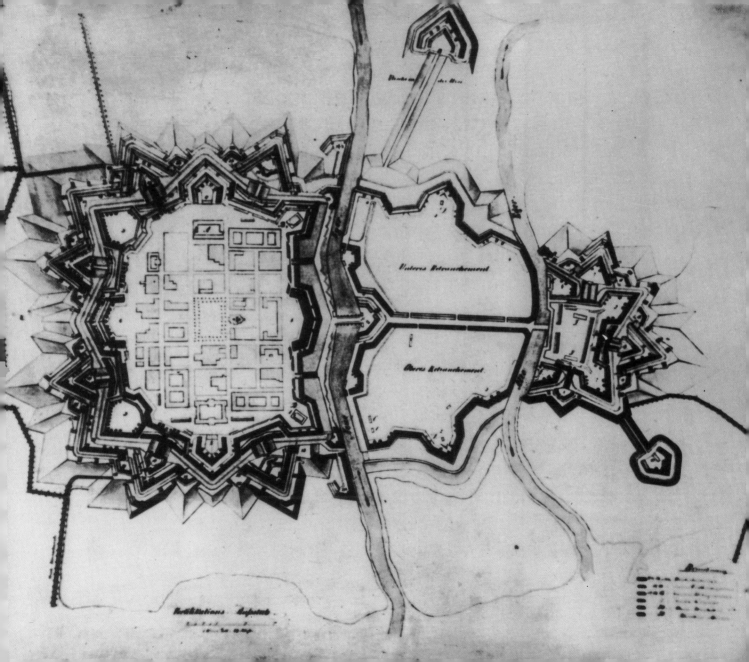

Unteres Retranchement

Oberes Retranchement

Fortifikations Aufriss

TEREZÍN is a word that will always evoke in us
  memories of war and death. The Terezín Ghetto is
  a symbol of cruelty and hopelessness.
Yet this book, which I am honored to introduce, is not
  itself a symbol of desolation, even though the prose
  and poetry in it was written in Terezín, during the war,
  at a time when Jews were being murdered in cold
  blood. Assembled with great care by the survivors,
  the texts in this book fill the reader with hope. It is
  an artefact that has emerged out of a longing for art. Art
  springs from truthful and extreme experience perhaps
  even more than it does from talent, and it has
  the capacity to be stronger than death.
The magazine *Vedem (In the Lead)*, produced by children
  living in Terezín under the constant threat
  of transport and death – the verses, stories, articles
  and other texts assembled here – are for us, who read
  it now, not only a memento of the horrors of the ghetto
  and of war, but an inspiration to live, and a measure
  of the pettiness of our present complaints. How many
  poets and writers left a record of their true birth here,
  in the shadow of death? How many of those young
  authors, had they survived, would have made the world
  a richer place?

Let us read carefully what the children of Terezín are
saying to us through their poems, their stories, and their
articles. Let us learn from them to have faith in truth,
love for our home and our homeland. Let us learn
firmness of conviction and courage to face the constant
presence of death.

Gratitude is due also to those who have survived and who,
mindful of their childhood friends, have overcome
the tremendous obstacles placed in their way over
the decades, so that they might preserve these rare
pages of *Vedem*, now half a century old. It is a proud
testimony to values that transcend time, death,
and destruction.

President of the Czech Republic

We Are Children

Just the Same

Vedem, the Secret Magazine
by the Boys of Terezín

Selected and edited by Marie Rút Křížková,

Kurt Jiří Kotouč, and Zdeněk Ornest

Translated from the Czech by R. Elizabeth Novak
Edited by Paul R. Wilson

With a Foreword by Václav Havel

The Jewish Publication Society
Philadelphia – Jerusalem

Contents

Foreword / 10

Dedication / 15

How This Book Came to Be Written / 16

TEREZÍN / 21

LONG LIVE THE REPUBLIC OF SHKID / 33

ONE OF US / 61

LIFE AND DEATH / 81

The Boys from Home One, House L 417 / 192

Epilogue / 194

Editor's Note / 197

Acknowledgments / 198

Dedication

What am I?
Who are my people,
Wandering child that I am?
Are ghetto walls my homeland?
Or is it a ripening land
Going somewhere, small, beauteous?
Is Bohemia my homeland, or the world?

These lines pose a question. It is an eternal question, one that seeks to find the meaning of life in an unjust world. It is all the more urgent since this poem, along with a few others, is the sole legacy of fourteen-year-old Hanuš Hachenburg, who died in Auschwitz in 1944.

And he was not alone.

He was not alone – these words, otherwise consoling, assume tragic significance here. He was not the only child prisoner in the Terezín Ghetto, and he was not the only one transported to Auschwitz. There were thousands like him.

The following pages record the fate of some of the hundreds of thirteen- to fifteen-year-old boys who passed through Home One in House L 417 in the Terezín Ghetto between 1942 and 1944. All but a few of them died. They perished together with their beloved leader, Professor Valtr Eisinger.

This book is dedicated to their memory.

How This Book Came to Be Written

Half a century has passed since the time we wrote and published our boys' magazine *Vedem* inside the Terezín Ghetto. Most of us were then deported to Auschwitz and other "final destinations." But fate is blind and, independent of our will, allowed some of us to survive. Astonished at the miracle of our liberation, we never dreamt that one of us had managed to preserve the magazine that had been the repository of our views on life inside and outside the camp, and our dreams of the future.

After the war, things turned out differently from what we had imagined. The official anti-Semitism that went along with the Communist takeover in Czechoslovakia in February 1948 was at times hidden, and on other occasions – especially during the political trials of the early fifties – blatant. It was this that prevented the publication of our youthful literary efforts from Terezín. Much later, in 1965, at a time some historians refer to as "the thaw," we managed to publish a lengthy account of *Vedem* in a literary magazine called *Plamen* (*The Flame*). With the coming of the Prague Spring in 1968, we began thinking seriously about publishing an anthology to include a portion, at least, of the material contained in the eight hundred pages of our magazine.

We were uncertain as to how to begin. Selecting the best of the many stories, essays and poems, all of which spoke to us directly in the intimate voices of our childhood friends, required objectivity. We were too closely involved with the magazine to be truly impartial. We were delighted therefore when Marie Rút Kŕížková agreed to become editor in 1971. She did so not only out of professional interest, as a writer, but also because she had a profound personal involvement with the subject matter.

In 1972, the Memorial of Terezín and the North Bohemian Publishing House signed a contract with us for this book. The manuscript was submitted to a reviewer, Dr. Václav Král. In his somewhat peculiar report, he managed to link the publishing of prose and poetry by children who had been interned in Terezín with "the aggression of the State of Israel against the Arab nations." Given the sort of thing that was going on in Czechoslovakia during the years of normalization (after the Soviet-led invasion in August, 1968) the reviewer's absurd attitude came as no surprise, and the book proposal was rejected. In a 1977 lawsuit against Ota Ornest, the brother of one of the editors of this book, the State Prosecutor declared that in sending literary texts abroad, including poems by the Nobel Prize winner Jaroslav Seifert and the manuscript of this book, Ornest had committed a socially harmful act. In 1978, the Paris-based Czech émigré journal *Svědectví* (*The Testimony*) printed excerpts from this manuscript along with a commentary on Ornest's trial.

Terezín was a gathering point for the entire Jewish population, especially those from the Czech lands, before they were deported to the extermination camps. The children of Terezín, as well as those from Warsaw, Łódź and other towns where they were imprisoned, form an infamous chapter in the history of anti-Semitism, and it was broad international awareness of the tragedy of the Jewish children that made the Communist ideologists and censors so wary of publishing this manuscript.

They were powerful enough to stop publication of the book, but they were powerless before human memory. They were powerless to stop exhibitions of drawings by the children of Terezín in many European and American cities. They were powerless to stop a visit by the French mime Marcel Marceau to Czechoslovakia in 1981 on the occasion of arrangements for the filming of *The Last Butterfly*, inspired by the fate of the children of Terezín, or the unveiling of a statue to the memory of these children by the Italian sculptor Emilio Greco. Though it was paid for by the Italian public, the Czechoslovak authorities did not allow Greco's monument to be erected in the former school of Terezín.

In 1968 attempts were made to convert the school building into a museum commemorating the Ghetto, but after the Soviet invasion of Czechoslovakia that August, the "normalizers" had a monstrous Museum of the State Police Force and the Revolutionary Traditions of the North Bohemian Region erected on its site instead. It was a grotesque achievement. Terezín became the only former concentration camp site immortalized for three decades as a police museum. It is only now that the museum originally intended for that location is being set up.

Thanks to the work done by Marie Rút Křížková, the manuscript of *We Are Children Just the Same* was published in 1978 as a "samizdat" (or self-published) book under the editorship of Jan Vladislav under the title *Are Ghetto Walls My Homeland?* This version was so well received that it was re-issued again in the late eighties, also in typewritten form, but in a different format and design. In this form, it was exhibited at the Frankfurt Book Fair in 1990.

In the present edition, some of the original text in the "samizdat" edition has been dropped in favor of more illustrations. These include not only original drawings from the magazine *Vedem* and documentary photographs, but also the artwork of other boys and girls interned in Terezín, most of whom were ten to twelve years old at the time, that is, two or three years younger than the authors of *Vedem*. They still looked upon the world with children's eyes, and their work gives the book a new and captivating dimension.

Zdeněk Ornest, who wrote a great deal in *Vedem* (especially poetry) and helped prepare this volume, died suddenly in the fall of 1990 and unfortunately did not live to see the result of his work published as a printed book.

As I leaf through *Vedem*, I recognize my own childish handwriting on some of its pages. The editor, our beloved Petr Ginz, compelled me to be the editorial factotum, to hound tardy contributors and then transcribe their work neatly for the final edition of the paper. He did not entrust the more important editorial jobs to me. Young as he was, his personality was already fully formed and he did not willingly let anyone encroach on what he considered his territory.

I can still see him, sitting cross-legged on his lower bunk, surrounded by pens, pencils, engravers, brushes and paints, and sheets of paper of all sizes, along with what was left of a parcel from his parents. Well, here you are, Petr. *Vedem* is coming out again. But it took us a long time, didn't it? Petr is smiling. "Mey-fah-zu," he says. He used to claim that this was an expression in the language of the proverbially apathetic Manchu people, which means, "There's nothing to be done about it." I still don't know if this is true, or whether Petr just made it up. I never had a chance to ask him. "Well, get on with it," he'd say. "Go round to all the boys so we get it out on time…"

"Right, Petr, I'm on my way…"

– Kurt Jiří Kotouč

Petr Ginz
(b. 1928, perished).
"Squares, areas…"
Pencil, 140 × 90 mm.
Jewish Museum, Prague,
Inv. No. 131969.

Terezín – an aerial view.
Jewish Museum, Prague,
Neg. No. 29633.

TEREZÍN

Terezín

A little dirt within the dirty walls
And round about a little bit of wire
And thirty thousand sleeping there,
Who will awake one day
And who see their life blood
Spilled around them.

I was a child once – two short years ago.
My youth was longing for another world.
I am a child no longer – I saw things to make me blush,
Now I am adult and have known terror,
Bloody words and murdered day.
That is no longer just a bugaboo!

But I also believe that I am only sleeping,
That I shall see my childhood once again,
Childhood like a wild, wild rose
Like a bell to wake me from my dreams,
Like a mother who, with womanly intuition,
Loves the naughty child most.
How terrible my youth that watches only
For the enemy, the rope.

How terrible a youth, that to itself
Must say: this one is good, and that one is evil.
Somewhere in the distance, childhood sweetly sleeps,
Along the narrow paths of Stromovka park,
There, from that house, someone leans out,
Where only contempt is left for me,
Where long ago, in gardens full of flowers,
My mother brought me into the world to weep.
In candlelight I sleep on my hard pallet,
And one day perhaps I shall understand
That I was just a tiny tiny creature,
As small
              as that chorus
                      of thirty thousand.

– Ha- (*Hanuš Hachenburg*)

Transport arriving in
Terezín.
Jewish Museum, Prague,
Neg. No. 24758.

* Bonkes is slang for rumor
  or gossip.

How I Came
to Terezín

On March 24, 1944, I had the honor of arriving in Terezín. To be precise, the train stopped at Bohušovice, not Terezín. A few gentlemen of the SS entered our train and grabbed us. We in turn grabbed our packs and then everything was thrown helter skelter onto a wagon pulled by a tractor. After a distressing trip accompanied by a cordon of gendarmes, who surrounded us to make sure that no one in the precious load of seventeen Jews was lost, we arrived at the infamous and almost legendary Terezín. Again gentlemen in uniform appeared and shouted something at us in German, and only later did I understand that they were strongly advising us to hand over our gold watches, money and suchlike if we valued our lives. Then they stripped us, searched us to see if we had really handed everything over, found a few things, took them away, and instead of giving the former owners a voucher, slapped their faces. And so we entered another world, ruled over by the Jews themselves – the infirmary in the Ústí barracks. We were checked for lice, or so the doctor said. Then he pumped a few cc's of anti-typhoid serum into us and we were dismissed into the ghetto. Accompanied by strange, self-important gentlemen, some with yellow bands round their black caps, we went to the delousing station. While the *Bademeisters* scrubbed and soaped us, they fired questions at us. They wanted to know what was new in Prague: are the coffee houses and shops closed? Is it true that the statue of St. Wenceslas has been demolished? Within the space of a few minutes we heard so much nonsense that our heads were spinning: these were the Terezín *bonkes*.* Finally, at 11 o'clock at night, they took us to the Hannover barracks where bunks were allotted to us. Sleeping was out of the question, because the alarm went off three times, and there were fleas and other vermin. That's about all I have to say about my arrival in Terezín.

– Cortez (*Unknown author*)

Two Dreams

Jaroslav Žák and Vlastimil Rada: "The Adventures of Děda Posleda." The voice of the storyteller is growing weaker, and finally I can only hear, as if from a distance, the adventures of the courageous old man and the Dusbálek family. But even that fades and, carried away in the arms of Morpheus, I find myself on the ramp in front of the National Museum in Prague overlooking Wenceslas Square. From high on the ramp, I admire the thousands of lights. The neon signs outside the newspaper offices of *České slovo* and *Národní politika*, the Prokop and Čáp department stores, and many more, seem to wink at me in a friendly way as I walk down the ramp and along one of the most beautiful boulevards in Prague. I reach the wide avenue at the bottom – our Broadway – Příkopy, and admire the splendor of the neon ads, the brightly lit coffeehouses and the theaters and cinemas where crowds of people are milling around, arriving in cars, or getting out at the nearest tram stops. When I have seen enough of this wonderful show, I walk away toward the Old Town Square. Prague's ancient astronomical clock is invisible up in the dark and, disappointed, I walk on to the Parliament buildings, where a great banquet seems to be in progress. A soldier on guard duty in front of the building, his uniform spotless and his boots shined to perfection, is saluting a gentleman in a top hat, probably some bigwig. I continue on my way and find myself on the banks of the Vltava river, where the lights reflected in the water remind me of the song: "Prague is so beautiful…"

Again I am standing on the ramp in front of the Museum, but how did this happen? I can no longer see any neon lights. Wenceslas Square is like a bottomless pit, dark and deserted. Only the silhouette of the statue of St. Wenceslas stands out against the darker sky. I walk down toward Příkopy, hoping that there, at least, I will find some of the former beauty. But suddenly I stop, rooted to the spot. Coming toward me are several young louts in black boots and they are stopping people, demanding to see their identity cards. When they are handed over, the people are beaten up! I look at the victims more closely and see that on their left breast they are wearing a yellow patch in the shape of a star. Involuntarily I look down at the left lapel of my own jacket – and oh horror! I too am wearing a yellow patch. The louts in the black boots have already reached me. They

are shouting at me … I wake up drenched in sweat.

"Gentlemen, for the last time, who is going to the doctor's infirmary? After this I won't take down any more names."

– Baked glasses (*Hanuš Kahn*)

Hanuš Kahn
(b. 1930, perished).
Drawing.
Pencil, 320 × 210 mm.
Jewish Museum, Prague,
Inv. No. 131216.

Hana Turnovská
(b. 1932, perished).
"Entering the Park
Prohibited."
Crayons, 310 × 220 mm.
Jewish Museum, Prague,
Inv. No. 131338.

Memories of Prague

How long since I last saw
The sun sink low behind Petřín Hill?
With tearful eyes I gazed at you, Prague,
Enveloped in your evening shadows.
How long since I last heard the pleasant rush of water
Over the weir in the Vltava river?
I have long since forgotten the bustling life on Wenceslas Square.
Those unknown corners in the Old Town,
Those shady nooks and sleepy canals,
How are they? They cannot be grieving for me
As I do for them. Almost a year has passed.
For almost a year I have huddled in this awful hole.
A few poor streets replace your priceless beauty.
Like a beast I am, imprisoned in a tiny cage.
Prague, you fairy tale in stone, how well I remember!

– nz (*Petr Ginz*)

Petr Ginz ?
(b. 1928, perished).
"Houses on the Bank."
Aquarelle, 150 × 220 mm.
Memorial of Terezín,
Vedem p. 129.

Two Recollections

Lightly, silently, the snow falls. Crystal flakes swirl through the air like dancers, slowly drifting down like a symbol of human life, to be joined on the ground by millions of others. It is one of the first days of winter, almost holiday-like with the coming of the first snow. Winter, it seems, has decided to enfold Prague in white robes to celebrate its arrival. I shake off my reverie and turn away from the snow-clad town. Suddenly I hear my mother's voice calling from the kitchen. "Hurry up, Rudy, you'll be late for school!" I hurry into the kitchen. There's a cup of steaming coffee on the table, with two buttered rolls beside it, baked to a golden brown. The room is warm and twice as pleasant with the north wind blowing outside. I quickly eat my breakfast, put my sandwich into my bag, don my coat and cap. A kiss for Mum and the door of our flat slams behind me.

The streets are still in half-darkness and full of snow melting under the feet of the passersby hurrying to work. From across the street a schoolmate beckons and we walk quickly to school together. Morning lessons are soon over and noisy crowds of boys and girls pour out of the school gates into the snow-covered streets. It has stopped snowing, the sun has come out and its warm face has transformed the city's white raiments into a sparkling cloak covered with thousands of diamonds. The air is clear, and everyone's soul seems uplifted. Many passersby break out in bright smiles when they see this snowy wonderland tempting the pupils, stiff with inactivity, to all sorts of mischief.

After an exhilarating snowball fight we hurry home, numb with cold. My parents are already waiting for me with a good hot meal. After lunch I stretch out for a while on the sofa where in the wink of an eye an exciting book transports me to faraway lands full of grand adventures. Suddenly I look at my watch: it's late. The boys will be waiting for me. I grab my skates, my hockey stick, then it's off to the ice rink with my gang. We are welcomed from far off by noise and shouting in the crystal winter air. Skates are donned and we circle on the hard, smooth ice, trying out the skills we learned the year before. Time spent in motion in the fresh air also passes quickly and late in the afternoon, tired but rosy-cheeked, we return home. At night I tumble into bed with memories of a wonderful day and plan the pleasures of tomorrow, until sleep comes and with it, wonderful dreams.

The door bangs. Zdeněk pushes breathlessly into the group of boys huddled in a corner. "The transports are leaving, gentlemen!"

"Great," says Erik sarcastically, and kicks the table.

"They say they're going to Birkenau," someone says.

"I heard it was to Třinec," replies another.

"So what, it's just more rumors." Bully, who is sitting on one of the bunks, is apathetic. "We've heard it all before, and it was always a false alarm. I say there's nothing to it."

"And I'm telling you, boys, that this time it's the real thing," says Kaki. "Dad says he talked to one of the fellows from the secretariat and he says this time it's really going."

"Oh dear," says Orče, taking his head in his hands, "then we're sure to go. We've been registered."

"Let's wait and see," Herbert responds, ending the discussion.

"Gentlemen, who is going for lunch?" And the group disperses, with each of the boys wondering, "Is the transport really leaving? And will I be on it?"

The noonhour passes in tense expectation. At two p.m. Honza bursts into the room: "Boys, the first lot is ready, I'm going to the *Leitung* to see who's in it." Pandemonium. A crowd of boys races to the office. There's a lineup there already. Everything is suddenly silent. All you can hear is the shuffling of feet. "A lot from Number Five are in it," someone whispers to the newcomers. The door opens. "Lustig, Blum, Polák Jan," says Ríša to those who are waiting outside, impatient, terrified, wanting to know the worst. "Kraus from Number One," we suddenly hear, and Hans Kraus comes out of the *Leitung*. He is pale but smiling and with an admirable mixture of despair and pride, he holds up his summons for the transport. Once you get it, it is really best to say: "So what, there is nothing to be done about it."

In a little while all the summonses have

Transport leaving from Terezín (Bohušovice). Jewish Museum, Prague, Neg. No. 24766.

been handed out and the crowd in front of the office disperses. "Gentlemen, I escaped the first lot, but I'll bet I'm in the second," says Orče, the pessimist, with a martyr's expression on his face.

The afternoon goes by in feverish preparations. In the evening, as luck would have it, there is a *lichtsperre** and we have to pack by candlelight, which casts fantastic shadows on the wall. "String!" calls Mrs. Laubová, who has the say in matters pertaining to packing. Immediately a dozen hands reach out with what she asked for. Suddenly there is a strong feeling of solidarity. Everyone wants to help. The second lot and any additions have not been announced yet. All at once, Tiny comes in: "To bed all of you, at once!" Everybody grumbles. Who can be thinking of sleep tonight? But in the end, everyone climbs into bed. I lie on my bunk and in my mind's eye I see a color film of Terezín. I see the *Schleuse*,** the pandemonium, the shouts and curses, then a sudden scarlet fever epidemic, the smell of medicines, fever, and then, half a year later, I am standing in the kitchen with a mess tin full of stinking, rotten potatoes, hunger again for lunch, every day, then the terror of being sent to Poland, and Mum's worried eyes when I have pneumonia. And my last thought before falling asleep is: What will tomorrow bring?

– ini (*Rudolf Laub*)

* Prohibition to switch on lights.
** Assembly point.

28

Untitled

Broken people,
Walking along the street.
The children are quite pale.
They have packs on their backs.
The transport is leaving for Poland.

Old ones go,
And young ones go.
Healthy ones go,
And sick ones go,
Not knowing if they will survive.
Transport "A" went,
And more went too.
Thousands died
And nothing helped.
The German weasel
Wants more and more blood.

– Klok (*Zdeněk Weinberger*)

Avowal

I know what depresses you, hurts you beyond belief,
Why you are lost in bottomless despair,
I know why life is crumbling beneath you,
Dragging you swiftly into gray oblivion.

I know you completely, I know your weak will,
I know your oversensitive ambition,
I know why only evil rolls his eyes at you,
And what riddles your face with bitterness.

We lived so well, as well as others did,
We had our freedom, each one had his treasures,
I know sweet fruit fell straight into our hands
And life wrapped us round with other things.

No cruel pitfalls, we were full of strength
We knew not misery, we knew not pain,
And now, now all that's left is dreams.
We wander blindly in a swamp, and who's to find us?

Why should we look for succor in the past?
Why should we fearfully turn our faces back?
Why rake the ashes of long rotted bones?
Why search for memories long lost?

Proudly we stand here with our throbbing wounds
We laugh and grin into the face of pain,
How could a pack of half-lies ever help us?
Let them not see our weakness and despair!

Look bravely forward, swallow all your sorrow,
Even though its bitterness might make us choke.
Do not be broken in this tattered labyrinth,
A dream will always end when we awake.

– Mustafa (*Zdeněk Ornest*)

From the Deposition
of Zeev Shek
Before the Commission
for the Concentration Camp
of Terezín,
June 29, 1946

Children:

… Hunger, harassment in the camps, mass executions, everything pales in the face of the terrible fate of our children.

The children came to Terezín in 1941 with the very first transports from Brno and Prague. Gonda Redlich and Fredy Hirsch, true to the tradition of the youth movement from which they came, immediately took charge of these children, and managed to arrange slightly better conditions for them. But soon the first separate rooms for the children were set up and later on in February 1942 the first separate Children's Homes. There were even a few people in the ghetto administration who understood the responsibility we had toward these children and who tried as best they could to ease their life in the ghetto. The main person in this was Jakub Edelstein. During the difficult discussion in the Council of Elders, when it had to be decided whose share was to be reduced and whose increased, Edelstein, through a courageous and clear analysis, swung the decision in favor of the children. This was perhaps somewhat unusual and cruel towards the older inmates, but given the times it was the only just solution: one made with the future in mind. … The Council of Elders' decision was applied in all the lodgings, in the kitchens and in the streets. Everywhere, special care was given to the children. They were given every possible advantage, and if it was possible at all to see a joyful sight in Terezín, it was children at play, children who looked relatively healthy and apparently carefree.

But anyone who worked with the children of Terezín knew full well that sometimes there was a strange light in the eyes of a child, a look full of so many "whys," to which no caretaker knew the answer. He knew that the children woke up at night, staring into the empty darkness, and he sometimes heard their quiet sobs, and knew there was no cure. He understood the complexity and the tragedy of a Jewish child's soul, though no psychology textbook existed to offer consolation.

And so life in the children's barracks evolved separately. According to the principles of collective education the individual rooms became separate "homes" that established their own daily timetable.

Jakub Edelstein
(1907–1944),
the first chairman of the
Council of Elders in the
Ghetto of Terezín. He tried
to improve living
conditions for the
imprisoned children and
teenagers.
Jewish Museum, Prague,
Neg. No. 5144.

Yet here, too, all efforts were in vain. The constant arrival and departure of transports, the regulations, the harassment – all this gave no peace to the children. In all, about fifteen thousand children passed through Terezín. Transport to the east meant death. In the beginning children up to the age of twelve could be protected. Gradually, however, the age limit was reduced and in October, 1944 even infants were sent off…

In the winter of 1944–1945 there were 1,086 children left in Terezín, and at the end of the war less than three hundred children over fourteen years old returned from the camps. Not a single child under fourteen, unless he or she was among the few lucky ones that had remained behind in Terezín, came back.

None of the effort, none of this collective care for the children's mental and physical welfare, none of the education, both individual and collective, bore fruit. It made the children's stay in the ghetto a little easier. It could not prevent their terrible fate.

VEDEM, Terezín 1943

Five

This morning at seven, so bright and so early
Five novels lay there, sewn up in a sack
Sewn up in a sack, like all of our lives,
They lay there, so silent, so silent all five.

Five books that flung back the curtain of silence,
Calling for freedom, and not for the world,
They're somebody's novels, someone who loves them....

They called out, they cried, they shed tears, and they pleaded
That they hadn't been finished, the pitiful five.

They declared to the world that the state trades in bodies
Then slowly they vanished and went out of sight.

They kept their eyes open, they looked for the world
But nothing they found. They were silent, all five.

– Academy (*Hanuš Hachenburg*)

Title page, *Vedem* No. 21, May 28, 1944, with a drawing of the symbol of Home One.
Pen, brush, ink, aquarelle, 204 × 300 mm.
Memorial of Terezín, *Vedem* p. 668.

-668-

Vedem

28. V. 1944 - 21. ČÍSLO - 2. ROČNÍK

Máme v úmyslu uveřejnit seriál článků o velkých
mužích všech národů všech dob. Než však uveřejním
první článek o indickém politikovi současném, Mahad-
ma gandhim, chci předeslat několik slov na vysvětlenou,
koho považuji za, velké" muže a proč o nich chci psát. —
Nečiním tak proto, že bych pěstoval kult velkých lidí, kteří
vynikají vysoko silou svého intelektu a ční vše nad obecný
průměr. Tento kult, přiznávám, je hodně rozšířený. Tisíce lidí
se sklánějí v obdivu i pse nad takovými, vůdci" — mluve-
no s Bedřichem Nietschem, kteří jsou většinou lidé nenávidí-
ce žíravila lidstva, jejich činy jsou svízelné úkoly proti blahu
lidstva. Tito lidé mi připadají jako ta písklata z Gottovy básně
jež byla zavražděna, že byla zašlapána nohou milované, ale surové
pasačky. A nejsou to jen slabá a malá individua, která se
vyznačují takovou slabostí charakteru a nedostatkem pevného
postoje a názoru životního. Nebyl to nikdo menší než Heinrich
Heine, který, ač horlivý demokrat a republikán ve všech svých
básnických projevech, se nemohl potlačit velký obdiv pro despotické-
ho Napoleona — Ne o takových velikánech dějin mluvit nebudeme
ač nelze jim odepřít velký dějinný význam. V dějinách zápasí-
ly a zápasí mezi sebou síly kladné a záporné. A obojí se soustřeďují do značné míry, než jsou uskutečňovány a organi-
zovány jednotlivci; jednotlivci silnými, charakterními, vysoký-
mi dary intelektu, vůle, citu a fantasie, kterými a povznášejí
vysoko nad své současníky. A záporné společenské síly, které
mnohdy po celá desítiletí, ba staletí vítězné odrážejí úkoly
sil kladných se soustřeďují pochopitelně v individualitách
po stránce duševní, rozumové a volně velmi pevně a silně
organisovaných. Jenže tyto individuality si nezasluhují našeho obdivu, nýbrž naopak, našeho kladného opovržení a dě-
jiny ty síly na nich vyplnit tu drásnou kletbu, kterou
vyslovil popěvač Heine: "Nebudiž na ně vzpomínáno. Ať jsou

LONG LIVE THE REPUBLIC OF SHKID

A school building in the ghetto, designated number L 417. We walked through the silent corridors, the three of us, Zdeněk, Kurt and Marie. It was a Sunday and the porter kindly showed us through the rooms that had become classrooms again, where our children are getting an education now – not for death but for life.

"In this building there were ten so-called "Heime." Every "home" had its own room, its name and number, its tutors, who were called *madrichim*," explain the former members of "Number One."

"Home Number One" is now a classroom for Grade One. There are flowers on a little table, pictures illustrating the alphabet hang on the walls, a huge abacus sits next to the blackboard. There are no traces of the past. Or almost none. The doors are the same, marked by the children's penknives, the wooden floorboards, which always had to be scrubbed on Saturdays, are worn in places, the high coal stove… and the memories… (Terezín 1971)

VEDEM, Terezín 1943

When Buddha Sleeps…

When Buddha sleeps, he sleeps peacefully. When the Madrich dreams, that is quite another matter, for his sleep is often disturbed by all kinds of sounds, articulate and inarticulate, human voices, groans, and animal sounds too, not to mention all sorts of cacophony – tonalities and orchestrations produced by instruments other than the vocal cords. But it was even worse for the sleeping, dreaming Madrich when his house was on night "hygiene" duty – or in plain language – latrine duty. Then the rhythm of his sleep was like Morse code, all stops and starts. Such was the case this Tuesday night. Every two hours the Madrich's sleep was interrupted by the stamping feet and chattering voices of the returning duty patrols, by the groans of those who were awakened for the next watch. To the unhappy Madrich, it was more like being in a medieval Spanish torture chamber than the well-run Home in L 417. That restless night he dreamt a most terrible dream — in installments.

Hell, described in all its horror by the divine Dante, is a terrible place, but it's a perfect family idyll compared with the sicha* of the Madrichim, during which Madrich Fatty** presented his most humble request to Tsar Tyf IV, Tyf the Terrible himself, who assumed the form of Oťas, or Dr. Jachnin, or Gonda Redlich, or another of our most important personages.

"I humbly bow before your great majesty, Tyf, in whose eyes I beg to find mercy and favor."

"What is it you wish, miserable worm. Open your sinful mouth and speak."

"Your Grace, I have but one favor to ask. I speak not for myself, a miserable little Madrich. I speak for the little children of Home Number One, innocent souls all and dear to my heart. Have pity on them, I beg of you."

"Peace, worm, peace! Worm from the family of dwarfs, tribe of the ever hungry, tell your ruler your wishes."

"My Lord, I wish nothing more than that you rename our house. Could we, perhaps, call it House No. 4597?"

"Miserable worm, are you making fun of your master? Do you not know that we are as gracious in our indulgence as we are terrible in our rage?"

"My Lord, let me embrace the red hot iron maiden, fling me upon a bed of glowing embers, but in your mercy, I pray you, grant my wish." Thunder seemed to reverberate through the hall as Tsar Tyf cleared his throat. He blew his nose into a sheet, and said, "Tell me then, what is the reason for this strange request? Never have I heard a stranger one!"

"Sir, Sir, Shagruboo*** is up for patrol duty and we can't get him out of bed."

Tiny shot up in bed, covered in sweat and cried out: "What, from his bed of glowing embers?"

"Oh no, sir, he just doesn't want to get up. He's on duty now."

"I see," the Madrich said knowingly, blinking his eyes and wiping the sweat from his brow. "Well, you'll have to drag him out. He has to go." Having said this, he crawled back under the covers to be tortured anew by his terrible dream.

"Great Tsar, Gosudar, hear me and judge whether we in Number One are not creatures truly worthy of your pity. If the order comes to send fifty boys to carry mattresses, coal or pieces of furniture, the call goes out for the boys from Number One. If rations, or Schonkost**** has to be fetched, Number One has to do it. If an inspection party comes to check on cleanliness, hygiene, the daily program, etc., where will they come without fail, in their clattering and, if you'll forgive me, filthy boots? To Number One. If the lavatory lady wants to warm her numb fingers, where does she go? To Number One. If the cleaning unit needs brooms for the toilet, where do they come to look for them? To

* Hebrew "session."
** Nickname of Valtr Eisinger.
*** Jiří Grünbaum's nickname, from Shammes Grünbaum.
**** From the German: an improved diet for convalescents.

34

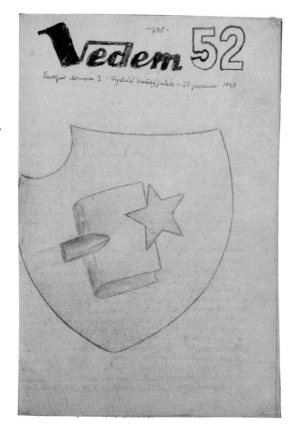

Number Two or Three, which are closer? No. There is an unerring, almost animal instinct in these old geezers that takes them straight to Number One. If the management wants to train a new Madrich, where do they send him? To Number One.

"Great Tsar, Little Father, Gosudar, please do not think that this is because Number One is a model Home. That has nothing to do with it at all. Kindly recall your own school days. Can you not remember how, when the teachers would test the pupils, they would always start at the beginning of the alphabet, with the result that those pupils were tested as often as ten times more than pupils at the end of the alphabet, who could carry on with their own amusements undisturbed?

"May I be boiled alive in your terrible steam caldron, and hung up to dry in a breeze

if all unwelcome visitors, inspectors, latrine patrols and other rabble would sooner cadge a cigarette off the Herr Lagerkommandant than enter our Home, if only Mr. Fischer would tell them our Home is Number 4597…"

At that moment Fatty, twisting and turning on his bed, heard a sweet voice whispering in his ear. It was Ríša: "Sir, here's an anti-typhoid pill for you."

I don't know what happened after that…

– Tiny (*Valtr Eisinger*)

Marie: Tiny, Fatty – I believe that's what you called the leader of your home, Professor Valtr Eisinger? Each of you had several nicknames. How did they come about?

Kurt: In various ways. Let's take Tiny. Professor Eisinger was not very tall.

Marie: In Number One you called yourselves the "Republic of Shkid." Was that your own idea?

Kurt: No it wasn't, was it, Zdeněk? Wasn't it Eisinger's?

Zdeněk: He used to tell us about a book called "The Republic of Shkid." He was very fond of it.

Marie: Did he read it to you?

Zdeněk: No, I myself only read it after the war. He merely told us about it, and it made such an impression on us that we all wanted to be Shkidovites. Shkid is really an acronym. It's from the Russian **shk***ola* **i***meni* **D***ostoyevskovo* – that was the name of a school for homeless orphans in post-revolutionary St. Petersburg. The book was written by two of the former inmates of the school – Byelykh and Panteleyev.

Marie: And they put together a magazine, or rather dozens of magazines, that started up and died again, and they gave each other nicknames, not just among themselves; they gave one to their director as well. I think they called him Vikniksor.

Zdeněk: Shkid was a secret. We had our own sign with the name Shkid engraved on it. It hung on the wall of our Home, but Eisinger advised us to explain this word to strangers as short for "Škola I. Domov (School first home)."

Marie: So you became a republic, and you were self-governing…

Kurt: And each one of us was responsible for something, depending on his interests and abilities. We set up our own government during a Friday evening celebration, on December 18, 1942, to be exact. We even sang the anthem of Shkid on that occasion. The chairman was Walter Roth, and he delivered the opening address. I'm sure Eisinger must have helped him put it together.

Address delivered by Walter Roth, printed in the "Political Review"

The banner has been raised. Home Number One has its own flag, the symbol of its future work and its future communal life. The Home has its own government. Why did we set it up? Because we no longer want to be an accidental group of boys, passively succumbing to the fate meted out to us. We want to create an active, mature society and through work and discipline transform our fate into a joyful, proud reality. They have unjustly uprooted us from the soil that nurtured us, from the work, the joys, and the culture from which our young lives should have drawn strength. They have only one aim in mind – to destroy us, not only physically but mentally and morally as well. Will they succeed? Never! Robbed of the sources of our culture, we shall create new ones. Separated from all that gave us pleasure, we shall build a new and joyously triumphant life! Cut off from a well-ordered society, we shall create a new life together, based on organization, voluntary discipline and mutual trust.

Torn from our people by this terrible evil, we shall not allow our hearts to be hardened by hatred and anger, but today and forever, our highest aim shall be love for our fellow men, and contempt for racial, religious and nationalist strife.

Prison lodging in the Hannover barracks. Memorial of Terezín, Inv. No. A 788.

Kurt: It may seem incredible, but the magazine was all our own idea. Professor Eisinger, and later on Pepek Stiassny, only wrote editorials. Every now and then Eisinger contributed a translation from the Russian, but that was all. Every Friday night we would sit around the table, or find room on the bunks, whatever, and then anyone who had written something during the week would read his contribution.

Marie: Why did you call your magazine *Vedem* – "In the Lead?"

Zdeněk: Home Number One was always first, Home Number One will always be so!

Marie: Ah, so that's it. And wasn't that your anthem, as well?

Kurt: No, the anthem was different. It was written by – no, it wasn't Eisinger, it was one of the boys who wrote it, but I'm not sure any more who it was. But maybe I can still remember the words:

> **"What joy is ours after the strife,**
> **In Number One we've made our bid.**
> **Self-government has come to life,**
> **Long live the Republic of Shkid."**

Sorry, I can't remember any more…

Zdeněk: Then there was a verse:

> **"Every person is our brother,**
> **Whether a Christian or a Jew,**
> **Proudly we are marching forward.**
> **The Republic of Shkid is me and you."**

It was sung to the tune of a workers' song: "Like a Tempest Round the World …"

Marie: I see you even put the price on the cover, sometimes 60 and sometimes 70 hellers.

Zdeněk: That was a game. The magazine was never actually published in the true sense of the word. We simply read it aloud every Friday night.

Milan Eisler
(b. 1932, survived).
Collage, 240 × 305 mm.
Jewish Museum, Prague,
Inv. No. 129967.

Marie: Wasn't that dangerous? I mean, to organize that sort of education in a concentration camp, with a flag, an anthem, a magazine, and everything?

Zdeněk: At the time we didn't fully appreciate what the consequences might have been. It was an adventure and it gave us at least an illusion of freedom. But it was certainly very, very dangerous for Eisinger.

VEDEM, Terezín 1943–1944

One of Us

Tiny:
To give you a faithful and detailed characterization of this rather plain-looking creature, it might be best to describe his activities on a normal day.

Let me begin with the first thing he does every morning. At about seven o'clock a call comes from his bunk: "Rise and shine, gentlemen, rise and shine!" Most of the crew of Number One respond by making sure that the cock has crowed only once, then they turn over and go back to sleep. This brings Tiny fully awake, and after a short deliberation he decides to crow once more. The result is nil, except that now Walter Roth has woken up and immediately starts a violent argument with Tiny, who decides to set a good example by getting up himself, crowing for the third time as he does so. Since this third call is usually no more successful, Tiny immediately becomes the teacher, grabs his notebook and announces, with a crafty smile, that he hasn't put the day's latrine detail together yet. The effect is instant. Except for a few poor jerks – who will end up on latrine duty – most of the boys vanish into the washroom or start jumping up and down on the beds to demonstrate that they are "up." The routine morning cleanup then proceeds, accompanied by a lot of commotion and several minor episodes such as "morning coffee-break at the Fischls" or "Ginz Ralf versus Aaron Mowgli." Tiny intervenes by shouting every now and then, but no one takes much notice. During the morning he inflicts his presence on the program committee, so you don't see much of him at Number One.

At midday, after lunch, he usually takes the roll call, which proceeds as follows: Tiny, having devoured his five lunches (teaching has its advantages), wipes his imaginary moustache, draws himself up to his full height – making him almost visible – and whistles with all his might. The only perceptible effect is that the noise level in the room drops by about a half a percent. "Are you deaf?" From this question the bright boys of Number One gather that he has probably whistled, and slowly but surely they begin to assemble in front of their bunks. "This has to stop!" mutters the man with the forehead of a peasant and begins to trot up and down the room. "All the duties I have allocated must be finished by the end of the week," he declares, to the merriment of those who happen to be listening, and he hears cracks like, "What optimism!" or "Who's he kidding?"

"Silence!" Tiny finally manages to shriek, stamping his tiny feet. He's nearly lost his voice. Now that he's got a little of their attention, he delivers another incoherent speech, the contents of which are familiar to all, dismisses the assembly, and runs to see Věra.

In the afternoon, if necessary, he appoints the remaining latrine details for the week, then he's gone. In the evening we only see him if there is something on the program. Otherwise he either claims that he has to go to choir practice and disappears (no one knows where he goes, though we have our suspicions) or he lies down on his bed. In this case there's a chance he might tell us one of his wonderful stories, such as "Jadérka in Front of the Cinema" or "seldom" told tales about his graduation.

That is all one can say about his daily activities in Number One, for his sleep is the sleep of the just, so there is nothing to write about him, let alone ridicule.

To conclude I would like to explain why I have written this article. It was at the last general meeting when Tiny, after a terrible argument about writing for the paper, sat quite dejectedly at the empty table, staring at nothing. I was in a jovial mood, so I approached him with the intention of getting at him with a stupid joke, the sort that Walter Roth likes to use against him. I said in honeyed tones:

"Just so you'll know, I intend to write something for the paper, but I'm going to make fun of you." I expected a gruff reply, but the tables were turned on me when the desperate teacher answered: "For Heaven's sake, write whatever you want, even about me, but at least write something!" And so I did.

– ini (*Rudolf Laub*)

Kurt: Eisinger's most impressive quality was his tolerance. He firmly believed in a new, socially just world order, but he did not expect us to mechanically accept his belief. On the contrary, he insisted that if we wanted to form an independent opinion at our age, we would first have to know a lot. And he practiced what he preached. For instance, he arranged for people with very different views to come to the Home and talk to us.

Zdeněk: Eisinger would never interfere with what they said. But after the talk he could wittily, in a few sentences, put everything in perspective.

Marie: Do you think that when he became the head of your Home, Eisinger expected you to become the most mature group in the whole school?

Kurt: I wouldn't say so. I think, rather, that in the end Eisinger himself was surprised at the way our Home developed. In the beginning, I don't think he'd set his sights so high. He just wanted to whip us boys into shape.

Marie: Did he choose his charges himself?

Zdeněk: We'd be overestimating ourselves if we thought he had. It was chance and age. The older boys were put into Numbers One and Five. If Eisinger had become the head, say, of Number Five, he probably would have achieved the same results there. His effectiveness came from a special inner strength. He was able to evoke things in others. He gained our complete trust. We were inspired by his tremendous altruism. He was never self-absorbed, he never lost his temper. We never had to wonder what had come over him.

Marie: What was an ordinary day like for the boys in L 417?

Kurt: Every day about forty boys went out to do various jobs in the ghetto. They were chosen from the two oldest houses, Numbers One and Five. From 1943 onwards, I too went to work. The work wasn't heavy; mostly we worked in

Unknown aritst
"The Hamburg Barracks."
Brush, aquarelle,
275 × 200 mm.
Memorial of Terezín,
Vedem – supplement after
p. 61.

the kitchen garden on the "Schanzen," the ramparts surrounding Terezín. At least we got outside. Our only supervisor was a Jewish gardener, a very pleasant young man we called Manci. I think his real name was Manuel. Every now and then we managed to steal a tomato or a kohlrabi. The gardening group was unique in another way too: to get to work they had to march a few hundred meters through "free territory," if you could call a road in the Protectorate free. In special cases boys were put to work elsewhere. George Brady was apprenticed to a plumber and Jan Boskovic to an electrician.

Marie: Did all the other children from Number One, Five and the other eight homes go to school?

Kurt: Yes, but only after a rather hectic and strenuous morning. Morning wake-up call was at six or seven o'clock. Then we washed under a dribble of cold tap water, and made our beds. After that the day's duties were assigned – for cleaning the rooms and corridors, the lavatories and the courtyard. Then came breakfast and roll call. All Homes fell in line in the corridor and the head of L 417, Otík Klein, read out the "daily orders." It was only then that classes started. Because of the shortage of space, classes were sometimes held right in the homes, but mainly they were held in the attics, where there was less danger that the SS would suddenly burst in on us. Whenever classes were held, some of the boys would be put on lookout duty. In case of an inspection by the SS, each form had to pretend to be doing something else, like cleaning the room.

Marie: Was the teaching systematic, according to a syllabus?

Kurt: Of the eight or ten teachers, only two or three were professionally trained. There were no teaching aids and the classes often contained children of different ages and very different previous schooling. Still, the teachers tried to maintain a certain system, and they consulted each other in what they called pedagogical councils. There were three or four hours of teaching a day. I can still remember my math, history and geography lessons. Hebrew was optional. Like children everywhere we were sometimes very naughty, but in spite of everything we completely accepted our teachers' maxim that we must keep up with the children in schools outside. Perhaps the best answer to your question is that the system was created not just by the teaching, but by the daily living together – the boys, the teachers and supervisors. I only realized how effective it had been when I came back from the concentration camp and attended a normal school again. I had not really fallen behind the others in any subject.

Marie: Were the children free to do what they wanted after school?

Kurt: After taking our mess tins to get lunch, which we had to line up for outside the kitchen in the Hamburg barracks, we reviewed what we had learned that day, without the teachers present. There could be other activities as well. The favorite was Physical Training, such as a football match in the yard. The most unpopular was "the big cleanup." The only real free time was in the late afternoon before supper, roughly between four and five o'clock. A number of children had parents in Terezín, or at least some relatives, and that was when they went to visit them in other barracks. After supper the Homes became worlds unto themselves, where the children, depending on their age and their supervisors' abilities, amused themselves before bedtime. In any case, in the younger homes lights-out was very early, but we older ones stayed up late. We also went to see the famous Terezín performances – cabarets, plays, recitals, and concerts. And I also remember the coal-stealing expeditions after dark, one of which very nearly finished me because I couldn't get back out of the cellar I was in. And of course the most "advanced" of the boys already had their eyes on the girls. After lights-out at ten o'clock we went on talking in our bunks for a long time, until even the most persistent were finally overcome by exhaustion and fell asleep.

I should explain that it wasn't usual for the pedagogues to live in the home with the boys. They had their own quarters in L 417. The fact that Eisinger decided to live with us and sleep in one of the three-tier bunks – just like one of us – says more about him than words can tell. Those were magic moments, always after nightfall, or after lights-out, when we would talk to each other from bunk to bunk... Eisinger was a wonderful storyteller. We could have listened to him for hours.

Zdeněk: Eisinger could really behave like a naughty boy, like "one of us." I remember one time shortly after my arrival at Number One (at first I was in Number Ten, but when I saw what it was like in Number One I did my damnedest to get transferred) we had decorated our living quarters to represent "Wenceslas Square," and there was a surprise inspection by the SS. We all had to stand at attention while Eisinger reported. The way he did it, we could hardly keep a straight face; with pure comic panache he made fun of those SS-men in front of us – we knew what he was doing, and were delighted that they weren't aware of it. Eisinger had won us over forever.

Valtr Eisinger
(1913–1945).
Provided by the authors.

VEDEM, Terezín 1942–1944

One of Us

Proper Name: Bruml, Jiří. Abscess. AAW 830. Cuts a ridiculous figure. We can see him, shuffling through the room, shirttails flapping behind him. One trouser leg is usually up, one down. On his feet he wears what we used to call accordions, that is, stockings fallen loose in folds around his ankles. Fly usually unbuttoned, his shirt collar likewise. A mound of fluff on his head, as though ashamed of its master.

So much for his appearance. Now as to the daily activities of this Abscess: he gets up in the morning and overturns the coffee pot. He has to wipe it up, but spends half an hour looking for a cloth and meanwhile the coffee dries up. When Bruml realizes this he scratches behind his right ear with his left hand and mutters something with an amazed look on his face. Then he goes to the washroom where he puts a little water on his fingers and then he goes out again. It's a foregone conclusion that he will step into the full dustpan. Ríša* happens to catch him doing it and orders him to open the window or shut the cupboard, whereupon he shuts the window and opens the cupboard. That's when Ríša gets really angry and Abscess disappears from view for some time.

– nz (*Petr Ginz*)

* Richard Meier, tutor.

40

View of the square from the former school of Terezín. The building on the right (with tower) was the SS headquarters. Photograph by Vlasta Gronská, 1972.

* From the Czech for a baby's pacifier.

Jiří Bruml, fourteen years old, spent two years in Terezín. On May 15, 1944, together with his mother, he was deported by the Dz transport to the so-called Czech "family camp" of Auschwitz-Birkenau. The Dz transport was one of the few transports that did not go through the selection process, in which some were immediately singled out for the gas chamber. Instead the people in it were to undergo six months' "quarantine" at the end of which loomed the Auschwitz gas chambers. But the "family camp" was liquidated before then, in July 1944, when all the "able-bodied" men and women were sent to the Reich to work. All the children up to the age of fourteen, and their mothers, died in the gas chambers between July 10–12.

Zdeněk: Jirka Bruml, a.k.a. Cuml,* was also called Abscess. He was the tragi-comic hero of Number One. I used to know him in Prague. We both went to the Hagibor – that was the only sports ground where we were allowed to play before deportation. At that time he was an athletic type, but in Terezín he was in a terrible state. He had a number of illnesses, after which he lost all his hair, and to make matters worse he had trouble pronouncing "r" properly. He was a luckless fellow, as clumsy as they come. We called him also "Untam." I remember an incident that captures him completely. Once, when we were still living in the Hamburg barracks, there were about fifty of us lined up at the pump, as usual. When it came Bruml's turn, he managed to soap himself all over, but the water was cut off before he could rinse himself off. After the war I learned from an acquaintance who was in Birkenau with Jirka Bruml that he died as he had lived – luckless.

Kurt: He was an unusual boy, extremely talented. In all the competitions or intelligence tests we held, he was always among the best. Of course, in those days we did not appreciate his abilities. The more primitive boys tormented Bruml one way or another all the time. Today I recall that with great sorrow.

VEDEM, Terezín 1942–1944

Intelligence Test

Thirty-three boys took part in the intelligence test this month. There were one hundred questions on all sorts of subjects and Bucháček came tops with 75 correct answers, "Associate Professor" was next with 74. Abscess got 73 right.

Here are a few howlers from the competition:

"Big Bertha"* is a name given to fat women.

Kosher are people who don't eat meat.

St. Wenceslas was murdered by his brother Prokop Holý**.

Flora*** is a church in Prague.

The author of *Quo Vadis* was Comenius.

St. Wenceslas was murdered by his grandmother.

Bamboo is a hollow stick.

The highest mountain range in Europe is the Himalayas.

These, and many more equally stupid figments of our imagination, had to be corrected by

– DrBe (*Walter Roth – Beno Kaufmann?*)

Interesting Dialogues of the Week

Dummy: What's new?

Bolshevik: It'll be all over in three weeks.

D: What makes you say that?

B: We started on a stick of salami today.

D: I don't get it. Have you heard any political news?

B: No, but we started a stick of salami we've been saving since we got to Terezín. That says a lot.

D: What does it say? I don't understand.

B: Come off it. If we start on a salami we've been hoarding for a year and a half, it's obviously going to be over soon.

(Seven a.m.: Dummy is in bed, asleep. Embryo reaches under his pillow. Dummy wakes up.)

Dummy: What's going on?

Embryo: I'm trying to catch fleas.

D: Can't you do that some other time?

E: There is no other time. You can only do it when they jump.

D: Just let me sleep.

E: I'm moving out of here. I'm going to join Erik Polák, so there.

D: (half asleep) Go right ahead.

E: (Pounces on the eiderdown and catches a flea.) Got it! (Crushes it and throws it under the bed.) But it's not the same one. It couldn't have jumped all the way from the pillow to here!

(*Unknown author*)

* A big German gun (named after Frau Bertha Krupp of the Krupp steel works), first used in the shelling of Paris in 1918.
** Successor of Žižka in the Hussite Wars.
*** A hotel in Prague.

Marta Kendeová
(b. 1930, perished).
Collage, 250 × 205 mm.
Jewish Museum, Prague,
Inv. No. 133436.

Marie: How did Professor Eisinger handle discipline?

Kurt: Here too Eisinger showed foresight and corrected bad behavior with the cooperation of the entire group. When Shkid was created, the main mischief-makers were energetic but unruly boys who found it hard to submit to any kind of authority. Walter Roth, for instance, was a unique case in Shkid – a boy with very rich parents and a lot of self-confidence. He was brought up at home in the knowledge that one day he would be a leader. Roth became the first chairman of the self-government and I think he played his part well in the first phase. But of course, as the self-government evolved, he eventually had to go.

Zdeněk: It was the same with Jirka Zappner. We called him the Kid with a Beard because he was physically more developed than any other boy in Number One. We admired him, partly because he was already shaving. It used to be an honor to be allowed to shave Jirka Zappner.

Kurt: I remember how impressed we were once when one of the beautiful girls we secretly worshiped came to see Zappner. She waited devotedly till Jirka had finished shaving and got ready, then they went away together. We were full of admiration and envy.

Zdeněk: Anyway, when the self-government was formed, Jirka Zappner, who was physically stronger than the others and had all the boys under his thumb because they were afraid of him, got a very important position. He was put in charge of maintaining order in the "home." It was a bit like making the poacher gamekeeper, but to tell you the truth, there was order.

Kurt: As the self-government progressed, these boys naturally dropped out and others came to the fore, boys like Leoš Marody or Hanuš Kahn, whom we would hardly have noticed under different circumstances. They were

quiet and unobtrusive, but their abilities were impressive. They first caught our attention in *Vedem*, and later on they got together and signed all their contributions with the common pseudonym "Academy." They were the most talented and morally most mature boys in Shkid. And that was characteristic of Shkid. It was a collective, where everybody found his place, not just the most talented, but even boys like Hanuš Kominík. We called him Komiňas or Baron Münchhausen. He was incapable of helping to shape the life of Shkid or the magazine, but he found his place all the same. For instance, the tall tales he told before we went to sleep – he was constantly surprising and entertaining us. He always told some absurd, fantastic tale....

Erika Stránská
(b. 1930, perished).
Collage, 150 × 230 mm.
Jewish Museum, Prague,
Inv. No. 133675.

Soňa Fischerová
(b. 1931, survived).
"View of the Sapper
Barracks in Terezín."
Aquarelle, 310 × 210 mm.
Jewish Museum, Prague,
Inv. No. 125513.

44

VEDEM, Terezín 1942–1944

One of Us

Baron Münchhausen, Ramses, Tučlas, Komiňas...

He is a winsome, chubby little fellow. He wears black trousers that almost come up to his neck and has a shock of blond hair. He's incredibly well-informed about the course of the war, knows exactly what the most important people have recently said, knows the precise number of deserters from Terezín. In short, he knows it all.

He can also spin wonderful tales from his childhood. He told us once how he saw a car drive past, and then saw it bounce down the steps to the river embankment, drive straight into the water, and on the other side it climbed up the steep hill to the Letná district. Then it waved its wings and flew majestically off toward Dejvice. He had hundreds of such wondrous tales to tell, mixing fact and fiction. But now he's become a terrible skirt-chaser. When his Lianka walks past the window he's so eager to see her he tears a hole in the blackout. But otherwise he's a fine fellow with a great sense of humor.

– nz (*Petr Ginz*)

One of Us

I see that this column, which used to be a great favorite with our readers, has been forgotten. So I'd like to bring it to life once more before it passes completely into oblivion. I'd like to write something about a small and somewhat chubby fellow called Hanuš Kominík. Since I don't own a paper factory I can't list all his nicknames, but here are a few: Whiskers, Texle, Morskey, Komiňas, and so on, and so forth. And now something about his daily life. I am sure every citizen here knows that Komínek is one of the best cobblers in Terezín. From early morning until late at night he sits at his bench, humming a song. His favorite is "There was an old woman and she had four apples ...," but sometimes he digresses into a German folk song: "Marody, hast du gewaschene Füsse, Marody, geh in die Konditorei."* Sometimes he finds a shoe lying about in the room, grabs it, takes it to pieces and uses the sole for one of his repair jobs. The victim to whom the shoe (now only the vestige of a shoe) belongs naturally complains: "You idiot, you're going to repair this shoe or else!" And Komiňas, who has a comeback for everything, replies: "My, but you're bright, and so full of the collective spirit, you primitive idiot. ..." That's usually as far as it gets, because even someone with nerves of steel would have a nervous breakdown under the onslaught.

This was a small excerpt from his great life. But to keep in his good books, I must declare in the end:

If you want to keep your feet
Ready for work, dry and neat,
Give your shoes to Komiňas,
He'll patch them up for all of us.

– Don (*Herbert Fischl*)

News

From the observatory at the top of the church spire, an interesting twentieth-century natural phenomenon was noticed. Every third day, between 4 and 7 p.m., a huge heavenly body hovers between the electric power station and L 417, thus preventing any power transmission. But some scientists, and above all the leader of the *Putzkolonne*,** deny the existence of this body and support their theory with the following fact: During the cleaning of the Magdeburg latrine, the leader of the Putzkolonne suddenly observed a huge monster that sucked electricity out of the wires with obvious satisfaction, thus making lighting impossible.

Two individuals exploited this to construct something that was supposed to be a carbide lamp, but was generally referred to by everybody as the Stink Machine because of the terrible stench it emitted. However, this excellent light source met with considerable resistance among the populace, which immediately split into two parties: The Protestant Union and the Carbide League... But look out, the supporters of carbide want only to arbitrarily destroy electric lights and replace them with garlanded carbide lamps. Propaganda posters from the Protestant Union are plastered all over the place, protesting against the Carbide League, but they couldn't care less and march through the town led by the happy inventor Arse Edison, jogging gaily along on the "Cold-blooded Horse."

The situation reached a climax during tax assessment, which had to be done by the light of a carbide lamp. It began to emit such an inhuman stench that the unfortunate clerks rushed to the window to get some fresh air, accompanied by the sarcastic laughter of Ab-

* "Marody, did you wash your feet? Marody, go to the sweet shop."
** Cleaning crew.

scess, who led the Protestants. Thus the Carbide League suffered another defeat. Still, you heroic defenders of carbide, do not lose hope. Believe in better times to come. Believe in God and the STINK MACHINE.

– Tsar (*Petr Lax*)

"Tsar" was the pseudonym of Petr Lax. "Cold-blooded Horse" was the nickname of George Brady, one of the few boys (and for a time the only one), who did physical work, in his case plumbing. His pal Kurt Kotouč recalls that he got his nickname because he courageously walked along a very high beam, and it was evidently he who brought the carbide lamp back from the plumber's workshop. "Arse Edison" is another "artisan" from Home Number One, the electrician Jan Boskovic.

VEDEM, Terezín 1942–1944

Boys, who knows what BROCOFEA means???

I tried for a long time to find out what might be hidden behind this mysterious word.

One fine evening, probably because he was already rather sleepy and not thinking very clearly anymore, a chap from 42 invited me to join their BROCOFEA. I had nothing to lose and so, like a bride before the altar, I immediately said a loud "Yes." For a few days nothing happened, but then one day, when we were given cake, I was just about to sink all my thirty-one teeth into it when somebody shouted desperately: "Don't eat it, don't eat it ..." I thought there must be rat poison in the cake – the one thing we have plenty of – when I was told, "You'll need it for BROCOFEA." Now I knew: BROCOFEA must be someone, perhaps a household god, that I was required to feed. Later on I discovered that for some time all my extra rations had been diverted to this mysterious BROCOFEA. At last I gathered my courage and, showing my ignorance, I asked what BROCOFEA really was. And I got an answer: it stood for The BROtherhood of COmmunal FEAsting.

There are several competing bodies like it in existence. They are clubs, consisting of several individuals who pool all their food so that at least once a week they can have a proper meal.

– nz, – yer (*Petr Ginz, with unknown author*)

The Most Famous Sayings of the Week

Embryo: Football is the best game, right after Monopoly.
Šnajer: The Ghettowache? Everyone gives them a punch in the mouth and then clears out.
Secret Agent Boskovic: What did they hand out to eat today?
Pepek: You have to imagine yourself as Robinson Crusoe.
Šnajer: Our House is heading for rack and ruin.

Quote of the Week

I was doing the watering and Honza Pollak ran under the water without my noticing.

– J.(*iří*) Volk

Quote

From the era of blood injections: "He's got to hit that vein in your backside, right?"

– Secret Agent Mojshe (*Jan Boskovic*)

Quote of the Week

Doctor: "Do you perspire frequently?"
Horse Löwy: "Yes, I do. Mostly my feet."

Equestrian Ballad

A mess tin name-tagged Löwy
Belonging to poor old Horse
Got lost for sure – not maybe
and with it his dinner's source.

Oatmeal rolls for dinner,
Poor Horsey is so weak,
No longer is he a winner
He'll have no oats to eat.

Lacoušek asks about him
And whispers in his ear
I love you lots, that is no whim
But no lunch, Horsey dear.

Go to the kitchen, Horsey,
And tell them of your sorrow.
You'll get another nosebag there,
And lots of oats tomorrow.

– Pidli (*Emanuel Mühlstein*)

"Horse" was the nickname of Leopold Löwy. The loss of food coupons was a frequent subject of literary and theatrical satire.

Marika Friedmannová
(b. 1932, perished).
Embroidery, aquarelle,
175 × 140 mm.
Jewish Museum, Prague,
Inv. No. 129787.

VEDEM, Terezín 1942–1944

Quote of the Week

I'm afraid to speak. I might say something stupid.

– Medic Šnajer (*Jiří Grünbaum*)

Quote of the Week

There's a big difference between the bones of a chicken and a human, despite the fact that both walk on two feet.

– Socialist Šnajer (*Jiří Grünbaum*)

Quote of the Week

I don't care whether I have a quote in the magazine or not!

– Šnajer (*Jiří Grünbaum*)

Praise and Blame

There were moments of great anxiety, moments of fear. Transport call-up papers are being delivered – whose turn will it be?

Fate chose a few individuals from our group. That is cruel. But how much more easily our comrades bore their departure when friends stood behind them, showed their readiness to help, and did what they could. We must mention the enthusiasm with which Kangaroo throws himself into his social work. Indeed, sometimes he is overeager, but he does it well, and to each trifle he manages to get for his charges, he adds a part of his heart.

I thank you in the name of those who are gone, but also in the name of those for whom the transport may still come. I thank you for all your help at this moment of great need.

– yer (*Unknown author*)

Motto: Destroy
Whatever You Can –
A Terezín Proverb?

I don't know why it is – perhaps the reaction to some injection, heaven knows, anything is possible here – but it's a proven thing: the inmates of our home (interestingly only those up to the age of fifteen) have been afflicted by a strange disease that, so far, has never occurred anywhere else. It's more or less painless, at least for those who are afflicted.

What's it like? Suddenly (the incubation period is very short) the patient feels an irresistible urge to destroy or disturb some part of Home L 417. Since it is my responsibility to care for the well-being of the Home and its furnishings – and I stress: the Home and its furnishings – I decided to seek out the particulars of what, for me, is a treacherous disease.

After detailed investigations I have come to the conclusion that people infected by this unknown virus respond in different ways. One might almost characterize it as a form of specialization. I would like to describe some of these areas for you, so that you can avoid them, if you are healthy, or discuss your own area with other specialists.

Some of those affected, for instance, carry things in such a clumsy manner that they break as many windows as possible. (Highly

Bedřich Hoffmann
(b. 1932, perished).
"Landscape."
Collage, 245 × 195 mm.
Jewish Museum, Prague,
Inv. No. 129444.

Just a Little Warmth

I envy you a little warmth, my friends,
When, numb with cold, I crawl out of my bed,
When nothing else but coldness could I feel
Still wrapt in all the lovely dreams I had.

No wish have I to wash under the cold tap
Slowly I drown, not in my shame, but filth.
Oh, lovely warmth, oh warmth so dearly purchased,
I want to warm myself in your kind lap.

And when at last, with heavy heart, I wake,
And know that I am starving, I would weep
For all the hope that I must now abandon.
I only want to sleep and sleep and sleep.

– Orče (*Zdeněk Ornest*)

* Youth Care Administration.

** Dr. Hans G. Adler (1910–1988), an outstanding personality in Prague German-Jewish culture. In 1942 he was deported to Terezín, later to Auschwitz. He emigrated in 1947 and settled in London. His postwar scholarly and literary work deals with the persecution of the Jews.

irresponsible, is it not, given the shortage of glass in the ghetto? Fool, you object, that's just why they're doing it. At least they'll have fresh air.)

Football is played exclusively in the corridors, and unless there is a conflicting program, it's played in the home as well. (What's wrong with dirty smudges on the walls?)

Who needs a wastepaper basket, when we have windows that give out onto the garden?

We steal the bulb from the cellar for our very own private night light. (Who cares if someone breaks his neck down there in the dark?)

Boys, I know a new game: if you stick enough potatoes down the washroom drains, you'll have a really neat flood there in no time. (You could, if you wanted, use millet, noodles, or some other food.)

Never take ashes all the way to the dump; take them to the pump or empty them between the doors.

If you see a good blackout blind anywhere, tear it down immediately. (Serious reprimands – twenty-eight so far – have been received by the *Jugendleitung*,* but so what?)

Broken dishes can be thrown down the toilet. (Then Dr. Jachnin has a lot of trouble finding new ones.)

It only takes a few seconds to ruin the lock to the gymnasium door.

Kicking down a bit of the corner wall is child's play for the expert.

Emptying the tar container is fun.

Mrs. Bachnerová got the corridor beautifully clean (poor woman, she had to use cold water), so don't hesitate to strew pieces of paper or dirty bandages about. It won't look so monotonous.

☐ ☐ ☐

I found many more areas of specialization, but this is enough for one article. Still, I'm an optimist and so I say: it's better than catching typhoid.

Off you go, boys, the north wall of our house is still spotless. Go to it, give me something to do.

– Technician-journalist (*Leo Demner*)

Marie: But this is no longer criticism from within your own ranks.

Kurt: No, Leo Demner was the superintendent of L 417. Dr. Jachnin worked with him; he was in charge of the furnishings, and of hygiene. I should also mention Ota Klein – we call him Otík in the magazine – who was the head of the entire L 417 house. We were in frequent contact with him. The most important representatives of the Youth Care unit (Jugendfürsorge) in Terezín were Egon Redlich and Fredy Hirsch. There were others who looked after us but to all intents and purposes remained anonymous. One "friend" of Number One, for instance, was the young Prague philosopher Hans Adler.** I would also like to mention Luise Fischerová, who had once worked for the Czechoslovak Red Cross. She was a sensitive and charming lady. In L 417, she mainly looked after the sick. It was she who woke me up in the middle of the night to tell me that my call-up papers for an "eastbound" transport had come. She broke the news compassionately, and then stayed with me and helped me with everything.

Marie: What were relations like between Valtr Eisinger, the heads of the other homes, and Ota Klein?

Zdeněk: As far as we could judge, they got on well. Eisinger talked most often with Ota Klein, although I don't think they were close friends. But they always had plenty to say to each other about their work and the problems posed by our education. Otík Klein also often took part in our Friday meetings. Altogether a lot of guests came to see us on Fridays, not only from L 417, but sometimes also from the Jugendfürsorge. A regular participant in the Friday night readings of *Vedem* was Eisinger's friend, Dr. Bruno Zwicker, a strong personality and representative of the Brno school of sociology. He was in charge of all the lessons for the young people in Terezín. Sometimes even Dr. Jachnin came; I recall that he rewarded the boys whose contributions he liked best with a lump of sugar.

Marie: Dr. Jachnin – didn't he become notorious for wanting to dismantle the shelves you each had at the head of his bed?

Zdeněk: Dr. Jachnin meant well, and he was right, it wasn't very hygienic, when we kept all our things right behind our heads – but this was our last bit of privacy, and we were very upset when they tried to take it away from us. But we wrote about that in our magazine.

A letter by **Hans Adler**, one of the friends and frequent guests in "Number One," L 417. Shortly after his return from the concentration camp – on August 10, 1945 – Adler wrote to Kurt Kotouč of his survival in Auschwitz and Langenstein, of the death of his wife and his intention to emigrate.

Poet, historian, sociologist, theologian, political scientist and philosopher, **Hans Günther Adler** (1910–1988) came from a Prague German-Jewish family. His mother tongue was German. He was formed by the multinational cultural tradition of Prague and Austria. After the war he settled in London. His scientific and literary work, such as the novels *Panorama* (1948), *The Invisible Wall* (1954), or the scholarly publications *Theresienstadt 1941–1945* (1955), *The Concealed Truth* (1958), and *The Manipulated Man* (1974), dealt with the persecution of the Jews. In contrast with most works dealing with this subject, his concentrated on the inner, spiritual affliction both of the persecuted and those who survived.

Dr. H. Adler.
T.č. zámek Štiřín
př. Kamenice u Strančic

10. 8. 45

Milý Kurte!

[handwritten letter in Czech cursive]

HA.

Attention All:
A reply
to Dr. Jachnin's proposal

We herewith submit our views on the matter of reorganizing our home. At our first plenary meeting Dr. Jachnin presented his plan.

    Reply: We admit, Dr. Jachnin, that your proposal is the most practical and hygienically appropriate. On the other hand, you will admit that we are also entitled to a little privacy, which in any case is so very limited here. When children all over the world have their own rooms, we have bunks 70 × 30 cm. They have their freedom, we live like chained dogs. Truly, then, in place of their closets full of toys, you must allow us to have at least half a meter of shelf space behind our heads. You must realize that we are still only children, like children everywhere else. We may be more mature, thanks to Terezín, but we are children just the same.

    We hope you will appreciate our arguments, just as we appreciate yours, and that we shall continue to understand each other. It is our wish and common hope to make the homes as cozy and as comfortable as possible.

– pner (*Jiří Zappner*)

Marie: In your magazine you often mention the boys of Number Five and their leader Arnošt Klauber, nicknamed Sloppy. How did the Number Five, who called themselves Dror – the Hebrew for "sparrow" – differ from Shkid?

Kurt: The leader of Number Five, Sloppy Klauber, together with Avi Fischer, led his home with the foundation of the future State of Israel in mind, toward awareness of a Jewish nation. I should also say that in Shkid we had more of an intellectual education, whereas in Number Five the stress was on esprit de corps and sport.

Zdeněk: Sloppy was an outstanding athlete. I don't mean to say that Eisinger didn't appreciate sport, not at all. Eisinger regularly played football in Terezín, with great encouragement and support from everyone in Shkid. But the boys from Dror trained harder than we did and beat us easily many times.

VEDEM, Terezín 1942–1944

Sport in Terezín

The yard of the Dresden barracks is crowded, packed so tight from the attic to the ground you couldn't fit a pin in. Fourteen players are running round the field. The match between *Kleiderkammer* and *Köche* (Clothing Supply – Cooks) is under way. *Kleiderkammer*'s left winger, Naci Fischer, attacks. The crowd hums with excitement. He comes in on the goal, he shoots, but the goalkeeper dives after the ball and stops it. A mighty round of applause. The teams attack and defend, back and forth, and excitement in the crowd reaches a fever pitch, when one team scores a goal on itself.

The match is over. The spectators walk back to their quarters, but lively discussions continue. Suddenly a question comes up: suppose a ghetto team were to play in the Czech championships? Yes, everybody agrees, it wouldn't be any better than the average division club, although many consider them worse. But what does it matter? In Terezín we live in a ghetto, separated from the rest of the world by a thick wall. *Kleiderkammer, Ghettowache, Köche* are teams of league standard, fighting for the championship of the ghetto. In spite of all the shortcomings of football in Terezín, I think that it also has some great advantages. Why are the mighty Sparta–Slavia matches played in Prague? So that the spectators can see good football? No, sport has become a source of income for hundreds of people, a livelihood for thousands. Promoters, the officials, the players, the referees, all make money at it. The clubs don't play to become the best, they play for the money. The referees are bribed and so are the players. And the players don't play out of loyalty to the club, but merely to make a living.

But here in the Terezín football league, what do players on the winning team receive? And what do the organizers of the match get, when the Dresden barracks are bursting with spectators? Nothing. Here they play with true élan for their club. They play for the sake of playing and not for money. I think you can see far more self-sacrifice here than anywhere else. In the *Kleiderkammer-Köche* match, Glückner started with inflammation of the middle ear and a high temperature, yet he was one of the best players on the field. During the Hagibor Prague-Vienna match the ball went out of bounds, but the referee whistled a corner kick for Hagibor. Prague's left wing Franta Leiner, good sportsman that he was, kicked the ball out of bounds.

If we can play like this here in Terezín, where the world is upside down, wouldn't it be possible elsewhere too? Just as some poets call for "art for art's sake," so we call for "sport for sport's sake and not for money."

– Academy (*Unknown author*)

When speaking of sport in Terezín we must mention Fredy Hirsch, who organized the sporting activities for all the young people.

Fredy Hirsch was deported to the "family camp" of Auschwitz-Birkenau in September 1943. Jindřich Kolben, who reached the "family camp" three months later, recalls in his letter from Munich of January 21, 1972:

"... For children up to the age of sixteen, it was Fredy Hirsch who looked after them with great devotion. He was exceptionally able and dedicated. When I got to the camp, he had already been working there three months. During that time he had managed to establish a center where children up to sixteen could spend the whole day, from the time they came from their blocks in the morning, till evening. He introduced some sort of school regime, which was strictly forbidden. He managed to get them slightly better rations, and it could be said that his center was the only place in Camp B II b (the *Familienlager*) where a little humanity was preserved. Furthermore the children's center was the only building where there was some sort of heating in the winter of 1943. For those of us who were a little older, it was an oasis and everyone tried to get there one way or another. I was only partly successful; for a short time (for about two months from February 1944 to March 1944) I managed to become an auxiliary helper (*Betreuer*) for a group of about ten children up to ten years old who had arrived in December 1943 and for lack of space in the children's block had to stay in a block for adults. Sometime later, when these small children were finally transferred to the children's block, I took charge of a group of about ten seventeen-year-olds and together we did maintenance and cleaning, heating and various other auxiliary work for the children's center. On March 7, 1944, everything came to an end. Fredy Hirsch's entire transport (that is, all the prisoners from the B II b camp who had come to Auschwitz in September 1943) were first sent to an isolation camp (B II a) and next morning they all went to the gas chambers. Of course we didn't know this for sure, but there were rumors that the SS had given Fredy the choice of leading the children to the gas chambers himself in exchange for his life, but he refused the offer and was said to have declared that he would not abandon his children. In short, they all vanished without trace. That also put an end to the oasis of humanity in Auschwitz."

Thus Jindřich Kolben. Mrs. Juliana Becková, the mother of one of the boys from Shkid, Hanuš Beck, a great favorite with us all, was also a prisoner in Auschwitz in March 1944. She recalls a rumor in their block that Fredy Hirsch and a few others had got hold of some weapons and tried to organize an uprising.

Fredy Hirsch (only a few people knew him by his proper name, Alfred) was completely trusted by the other prisoners in the Czech family camp in Auschwitz. This is why he was to become the leader of the intended uprising, prepared in conjunction with the Czech camp by the *Sonderkommando*. (These were the prisoners who worked at the crematorium. They had practically no chance of survival because after a certain time they were murdered by the Nazis and replaced by newcomers.) Accurate reports of the murder of the September transport on March 8, 1944, and of Fredy's end, were submitted by two Slovak Jewish prisoners, Alfred Wetzler and Rudolf Rosenberg-Vrba, who managed to escape from Birkenau in May, 1944. With the help of the Papal Nuncio in Bratislava their lengthy testimony was sent to Switzerland and published the same year. One of them was in touch with Hirsch as the contact man in his resistance cell. At the decisive moment, however, perhaps out of consideration for the children, Fredy ignored his warning and allowed himself be transferred, along with the other prisoners of the September transports, to the isolation camp. He believed the SS men when they said that all the prisoners would be transferred to the camp in Heydenbreck. On the night of the 8th and 9th of March, when the trucks carrying 3,700 men, women, and children from Terezín did not take the turn toward the gates of Birkenau, but drove instead to the crematorium, he realized his mistake and swallowed the poison he always carried with him.

Fredy Hirsch
(1916–1944).
Jewish Museum, Prague,
Neg. No. 30034.

A Parcel

It was the wish of every prisoner in Terezín, first, that sof* would soon come, and second, that he would get a parcel. The former must be left to fate, so we shall deal with the latter. Let us look at how such a parcel comes into being. It is a long, long story. First we must get a summons to the transport department for permission to send a *Zulassungsmarke*.** Next, we send this to a relative, or an acquaintance who is only part Jewish. When the poor wretch gets the stamp, he can do two things. Either he says to himself that he hasn't got the money to go looking for things in short supply, and sells the stamp to somebody else for a high price. In this case, of course, the poor inmate of Terezín can wait an eternity, and his dream will never be fulfilled. Or, the adventurous benefactor may start looking for something to send. There are two ways he can do this. Either he will start looking for "nebbich" goods, that is, bread, potatoes, horseradish, or such like, or (what luck for the poor chap in the ghetto) he can take a lot of trouble over the parcel and track down dripping, butter, flour, etc. When this ceremony (the hunt) is over, he must pack that parcel. Naturally, that has to be done with great care, for God forbid the parcel should come open on its way. Then he posts it, and his task is done. As soon as the happy recipient in the ghetto gets his notification, he gathers a platoon of men to come and help him. At the post office he gets in line, and when his turn comes he pays his fifty crowns*** and he receives his parcel, full of joy at the size of it. Once home, he immediately flings himself upon the contents and, with Epicurean delight, gobbles up the various delicacies and sings the praise of the people who took pity on him. He sends off a letter of thanks in the hope that very soon he won't have to accept gifts from strangers and that he will be a free man again.

– Don Herberto (*Herbert Fischl*)

Petr Ginz
(b. 1928, perished). "Sunflowers." Aquarelle, 145 × 210 mm. Provided by Petr's sister Eva Ginzová-Pressburgerová, Beersheva, Israel. Photograph by Naomi Salmon.

VEDEM, Terezín 1942–1944

Morning Song

I picked a small forget-me-not
And kissed it, oh so tenderly.
The sun bathed in blood, searing hot
Before shining on the world so longingly.

Tender forget-me-not in your blue robe,
Growing high upon the steepest rock,
Know you not that on our haunted globe
The blood-soaked sun can only rise to mock?

(*Unknown author*)

* Hebrew for "end," in this case the end of the war.
** Admission stamp.
*** Valueless ghetto money.

The Future

Applause fills the hall;
The curtain's black veil,
Folded in waiting, will soon part.

A ray of expectation shadows the darkness around.
Lulled by wonders yet to come, the crowd
Slowly bow their heads. A tremor passes through them.

They are dreaming of the next thing,
How the world will bring them a goose,
The universe bow and submit to their "Ego."
Meanwhile the action goes on, whistling across the stage
And the crowd, food on its mind, purses its lips.

– Academy (*Hanuš Hachenburg*)

Only for Strong Nerves,
or The Events of One Night

What I am going to tell you really happened, and if some of it seems a little strange, believe me, it is true to the very last word.

But let me begin:

A few days ago, I woke up in the middle of the night, opened my eyes, and looked round. I could see nothing anywhere. The darkness was so thick, you could cut it with a knife. Every window was properly blacked out and the night light was not on either. And as I sat there in the dark, I thought, "This is the perfect time to play a prank on someone." God knows which evil imp put that idea into my head, but since with me, it's never far from the idea to the act, I put my slippers on in a flash, carefully climbed down the ladder and, groping my way in the dark, tiptoed in the direction of – God knows why – Ginz.

I was in luck. The moon was bright outside and a narrow strip of light came through a tiny slit in the blackout, casting a weak shaft of light on Petrushka's head and a part of the shelf behind him. I was just bending over him when I heard a slight rustling noise. I looked up to the shelf – and lo and behold – a tiny gray mouse with gleaming eyes looked out from behind a box. I held my breath, crouched as low as I could and waited, curious to know how this would turn out. The mouse looked round carefully, then, hop, hop, it jumped forward, raised its little snout as though it were trying to catch a scent, and then made a slight noise that sounded like: "Phee!" There was another rustling sound and a second mouse appeared. "Well, well," said the first one in a human voice. "You here already?"

"It's like this," the other replied. "I fell asleep here late last night, and when I woke up about an hour ago I found myself with a book on top of me. I had a look, and what do you suppose it was, Amelia?"

The first mouse raised its ears inquisitively and the other continued: "An atlas!"

"My word," said the first one. "It must have been quite a treat."

"You're telling me. I've only been at it an hour and already I've eaten the whole Union of South Africa, including its mandates." It smacked its lips appreciatively.

"Look here," the first one squeaked. "Petrushka got a parcel today, now that will be a treat."

"Yes, indeed," the second one sighed. "There are slim pickings in Terezín."

Then hop, hop, both of them disappeared inside the parcel. "Oh, a lemon," I heard one of them peep. After that, all I could hear was the sound of satisfied munching.

It was only then I realized that I was shivering with cold, so I quickly crawled back into bed. But I lay awake until dawn, thinking of what I had just seen.

– The Saint (*Kurt Kotouč*)

Marie: You were both hauled off to Auschwitz with the autumn liquidation transports in 1944. When did you next encounter *Vedem*?

Zdeněk: I recall reading our magazine just after the war was over. But then I gave it back again to Zdeněk Taussig, who had only lent it to me.

Kurt: I got the magazine in 1948 from my pal George Brady from "Number One" just before he emigrated. I can't say for sure who he got it from. It might have been Mrs. Laubová, who helped us transcribe the manuscripts.

Mrs. Laubová was a helper in "Number One." Her son Rudolf was one of the Shkid members and one of the contributors to *Vedem*.

I turned to Mrs. Brodová, a clerk in the registry of the Jewish Community in Prague, and she gave me the following information: Markéta Laubová and her son Rudolf were sent to Auschwitz in December 18, 1943, in the Ds transport. Everyone was imprisoned in the "family camp" in Auschwitz-Birkenau. The time and place of Rudolf's death is unknown, but his mother survived. Her name is now Fischerová and she lives in São Paolo, Brazil.

So much for the theory that Mrs. Laubová had brought the magazine from Terezín to Prague. It was obvious that the magazine could have been saved only by someone who had remained in Terezín till the end of the war. Then I was given another valuable piece of information by Mrs. Brodová. The only Shkid member to survive the war in Terezín was Zdeněk Taussig. All we could find out about him was that he was living somewhere abroad. Searching for George Brady seemed more likely to bear fruit, since we knew at least that he was living somewhere in Canada. I asked a friend of mine in Canada for help, and indeed, not quite a month later I got an answer with an address. I wrote, and in two weeks I had a reply from George Brady himself.

Petr Ginz
(b. 1928, perished).
"Terezín Lodgings."
Aquarelle, 145 × 210 mm.
Provided by Petr's sister
Eva Ginzová-
Pressburgerová,
Beersheva, Israel.
Photograph by Naomi
Salmon.

Excerpt from George Brady's letter

Toronto, January 25, 1972

Zdeněk Taussig gave me the magazine after the war. And since the world is a small place, about eight years ago we were working for two Canadian builders on a site in Hamilton, sixty kilometers from Toronto. One of them told me that his wife was Czech, and when he introduced us she said that we'd once been on a "double date" together in Prague, and that she was Zdeněk Taussig's sister. I phoned her last night, but she was out and her husband gave me Zdeněk Taussig's number. I rang him immediately and spoke to him for the first time in twenty-five years. He was quite surprised too. I told him I would send him a copy of your letter, which I did, and he promised to fill in all the gaps.

A week later a letter came from Zdeněk Taussig, New York.

Petr Ginz
(b. 1928, perished).
"Terezín at Night."
Pencil, 145 × 210 mm.
Provided by Petr's sister
Eva Ginzová-
Pressburgerová,
Beersheva, Israel.
Photograph by Naomi
Salmon.

Kurt Kotouč a Zdeněk
Taussig, New York 1990.

Anna Grünwaldová
(b. 1930, perished).
Collage, 190 × 130 mm.
Jewish Museum, Prague,
Inv. No. 125722.

Excerpt from Zdeněk Taussig's letter

New York, January 29, 1972

It was I who brought the magazine *Vedem* from
Terezín to Prague, since I was the only one in
our Home who had remained in Terezín
throughout. The magazine was hidden in the
blacksmith shop behind the Magdeburg barracks, where I moved when our Home was dis-
solved. My father was a blacksmith in this shop
and we converted the coal bin into a little room
where the two of us slept. I was driving horses
for farm work, and once or twice a week I drove
the corpses to the crematorium near Bohušovice. Towards the end of the war I took my two
horses, collected my family who had remained
in Terezín thanks to the fact that my father was
the only Jewish smith who knew how to shoe
horses, and we drove to Prague-Střešovice.

After the war I tried to get in touch with comrades who had lived with me in the "Republic
of Shkid" so we could decide what to do with
our magazine. Since most of the boys were in
the orphanage in Belgická Street in Vinohrady,
I gave them the magazine. I can't remember any
more to whom I gave it. I think it was Zdeněk
Ornest, who was my partner in the bunk in
"Number One."

20. VIII.

Barackenbau.

Před několika týdny jsem byl předvolán na pracovní úřad, jednalo se o práci na kamenku, planýrování Hütnice u Litoměřic, práce s krumpáčem a lopatou. Nástup práce byl v 6¹⁵ na dvoře v Sudetech, kam se pracovní skupina vrátí večer po 6 hodině, pracovní místo je vzdáleno 6 km, cesta tam a zpět 12 km, 3 hodiny chůze. Měl jsem tehdy večerní, typicky terezínské večerní teploty, 37²⁰ – 37⁸⁰, což se u mne projevovalo malátností. Podal jsem o kontrolní lékařskou prohlídku, při které bylo vyšetřujícím lékařem zjištěno, že jsem 187 cm vysoký, vážím 64 kg a mám zvýšenou teplotu (ve 4ʰ odpoledne) 37⁶⁰.   Doktor: „Srdce a plíce v naprostém pořádku. Máte nějaké zvláštní potíže?" – Předvolaný: „Večerní teploty, únava, celková malátnost." – Doktor: „Já mám také večerní teploty, a přece" – zde zvýšil lékař hlas – „pracuji!" – Usmál jsem se nepatrně, když jsem pohlédl na „práci" doktora rozvaleného v křesle za konfereničním stolem v chladné místnosti a přirovnal ji k 12 hodinám v červencovém tropickém vedru, 3 ho pochodu a práci s krumpáčem a lopatou. Odvětil jsem, že je jakýsi rozdíl mezi „duševní" a tělesnou prací. Doktor s nepřítomným pohledem na můj vyhledlou holandskou bředu, řekl s klidem a bohorovností nemocenského lékaře: „Práce schopen. Další." – Opustil jsem tehdy s hlubokou úlekou a pevně rozhodnut, že za žádných okolností nenastoupímватýní kontrolní lékařské služby pro pracující. Byl jsem tehdy přesvědčen, že doktor je ovšem smutně proslulý typ lékaře, nemocenského lékaře, který není schopnějšia soucitnější, který klesne uštěr dříve, než spustí budovu nemocenské pojišťovny.

ONE OF US

VEDEM, Terezín 1943

One of Us
Petr Ginz

In Terezín there was a little house, L 417, and in this house there was Home One, and in this Home there lived a little boy and his name was Petr Ginz. By profession, he is editor of the magazine *Vedem*. Otherwise, he is a private teacher of general sciences and an admirer of the great Zwikenneis.* As an ardent Czech he carefully corrects every spelling or grammar mistake, and is particularly keen on the proper use of the possessive pronouns.

By nature he is a malicious creature and loves to poke fun at his fellow citizens. Petr receives at least two parcels almost every day. He's just enjoying one of them now, and his bunk is covered with all sorts of things. Eggshells are strewn over the new number of *Vedem*, there are two lemons on the unfinished diploma, and a book from the lending library is surrounded by biscuits, pancakes and buns. Mr. Fišer enters and calls out the names of the lucky ones who have received parcels: Pollak Erik, Löwy, Ginz. Ginz jumps up and rushes to Podmokly,** leaving everything scattered on his bunk.

But Mr. Fišer grabs him by the tails of his hubertus coat and shouts: "For God's sake, you've got to sign this. …" The breathless editor backs up about ten meters (approximates the length of his coattails), quickly signs his name and a minute later he's in the *Zeughaus*.*** Eventually he returns, loaded down with parcels. But oh, oh, everything on his bunk has disappeared. After a long search, half of it is found on Orče's bed, where it arrived via the force of gravity; the other half is usually in the attic or the garden. But that does not worry Petr. He shrugs his shoulders and opens his new parcel.

– Abscess (*Jiří Bruml*)

Marie: You once wrote about Petr in the "One of Us" column. What would you say about him today, after an interval of thirty years?

Kurt: First of all, these texts don't fully capture our relationship with Petr. He was a boy everybody just had to like. True, he was often the butt of our jokes, as many others were, but everybody appreciated his abilities.

Zdeněk: You know, Kurt, I think there was a lot of normal boyish envy in this leg-pulling. Petr was the only one whose parents were still in Prague. On the one hand, that meant that he was alone in Terezín, but on the other hand he was constantly getting parcels. The rest of us, who got a parcel once in a blue moon, if at all, couldn't help feeling envious. I slept on the bunk below Petr, and I must admit I often suffered. …

Kurt: But I have to say that Petr shared his things willingly. He was altogether a wonderful fellow. I can still see him, sitting cross-legged on his bunk, always busy with something. He was either working on a new number of the magazine, or opening his latest parcel.

Marie: I can't understand how Petr managed to get so many parcels. My impression was that parcels could only be sent to Terezín with special permission, which wasn't that often.

Kurt: That's right. The parcels were an extraordinary thing. Hardly any of us ever got one because we no longer had any relatives in the Protectorate. Often we didn't even have anyone to write to. And that provided an opportunity for boys who did have relatives: they could send a letter or a voucher for parcels that could be sent under another name.

Unknown artist
Illustration to Jiří Bruml's article "About One of Us" (Petr Ginz preparing *Vedem* for publication). Brush, aquarelle, 90 × 65 mm. Memorial of Terezín, *Vedem* p. 81.

* Dr. Zwicker.
** The Podmokly barracks.
*** The former armory near the Podmokly barracks.

VEDEM, Terezín 1943

An Unsuccessful Ramble Through Terezín

– Hells, bells, it's already half past eleven, we have to start printing soon, and I haven't got my "Rambles" column yet, I said to myself. Where could I go to get an article of about ten inches out of it?

Just then the nurse came out of the sick bay asking for five people to go and fetch the *Schonkost* (special diet). She had four on the detail already and needed a fifth – quickly. So – what about you? And of course, I submitted to my fate and went (modeling my behavior on the great Leoš Demner). It was better than getting typhoid, and perhaps I might even get a column out of it.

When the nurse had gathered us all together, she brought some containers and said in a deadly serious voice: This container is for the special diet, and this is for the *Icterkost*.* You put the soup into this one, the mashed potatoes into this one, and the sugar beets into this. Then she went off to get the mess tins. We thought if we could sample a little from each of the dishes we might eat our fill. Kotouč** even suggested we establish a Dipico (dietary pinching company).

At last we set out. The journey was uneventful and we reached the Hamburg barracks, where the dietary kitchen is now situated, without mishap. Recalling my newspaper duties, I tried to get some sort of interview going.

– How many people does this kitchen serve?

– Why do you ask?

– If you want to know, I'm the editor of a magazine called *Vedem*.

– That's a good one – an editor – ho, ho, ho. Well, if you must know, about 450. Just look at him – an editor indeed, ho, ho, ho.

That kind of conversation was certainly not to my taste and so I took the container of mashed potatoes and left. We fell in and started back. Oh, what pen could describe our sufferings on this arduous pilgrimage! The wind drove sand into our faces, soup spilled from the buckets over our clothes and into our shoes, while the nurse, who wasn't carrying anything, quickly led the way. Kalíšek was pleased. His feet were warm, he said, because hot soup was slushing about in his shoes. Metzl said genially that no one would notice we'd spilled any soup. The wind was blowing sand into it anyway, so it came to the same thing. Komiňas complained about his hernia and Kotouč stoically bore his fate – a pot of gravy, part of which had spilled over his trousers. When we came to the end of our journey, we were exhausted both physically and mentally. We dropped our containers, turned around, and marched home. On the way a boy asked us what the people with special diet were getting for lunch.

– Sprinkled mashed potatoes, we answered.

– Sprinkled? said the boy, astonished.

– Yes, we answered, sprinkled with sand.

– nz (*Petr Ginz*)

Marie: I am constantly amazed that as thirteen- and fourteen-year-old boys, you were so persistent. Over the course of two years, an issue of *Vedem* appeared every Friday.

Kurt: That was entirely thanks to our editor, Petr Ginz.

Marie: Your leaders were elected. Was the editor elected too?

Kurt: No, I don't think so.

Zdeněk: No, Petr took the job on himself. That was certainly an expression of his dedication and willingness. And no one ever tried to take the job away from him. Even in Terezín it was easier to shirk.

Kurt: I think Petr was eminently suited for the job. He brought all the right qualities with him from home. His parents had obviously helped him to develop his talents. He was an extremely bright boy. He was a year older than the rest of us and I think he had had some experience in editing a magazine in Prague.

Marie: And how did Petr get contributors?

Kurt: That was tough. He extracted contributions any way he could. He browbeat, he appealed to people's consciences, and sometimes, to save the situation, he wrote the entire issue himself under various pseudonyms. He was completely wrapped up in the work.

Zdeněk: And Petr also had other more attractive means of forcing lazy authors to work. He wheedled out contributions in exchange for things he got in his parcels from home. The magazine was a matter of personal pride. He devoted all his time to it. Every day, all week long, he worked on the next issue. It was incredibly hard work, especially when you think that, with help from volunteers – and I think Kurt Kotouč was the only one – he transcribed all the contributions by hand.

Terezín 1944

From Petr Ginz's Terezín Diary

(This diary still exists. Before he was deported to Auschwitz Petr gave it to his younger sister Eva, who survived the war in Terezín.)

From February 8 to ? (Let it be soon):

After considering the matter for a long time, I have decided to keep a diary. I am doing this for Mummy, Daddy, and Eva, to whom I can't write everything I would like in my letters, because first of all, it isn't allowed, and second, I don't know German well enough. And then I'm writing it for myself, so as not to forget the many events and types of people I've come in contact with.

February 8, 1944:

I lie in bed. Next to me on the bunk are my neighbors Kalíšek and Cuml. They are talking about a boy who said, out loud, in a cafe: "Just look at that bald pate. It's smooth enough for a flea to skate on," and the gentleman who belonged to that bald pate spoke to the manager of the cafe, and there was hell to pay.

February 8, 1944:

... Then I went home, just in time to write a composition on the following choice of topics: 1. The life of an inanimate object;

Petr Ginz
(b. 1928, perished).
Illustration to his serial
"The Cunning Drews."
Pencil, brush, aquarelle,
180 × 204 mm.
Memorial of Terezín,
Vedem p. 112.

Dobyvatelé!

Muži statečných srdcí
muži slov a skutků
muži zbrázděných lící,
vy čistí, bez předsudků,
vy, již jste mřeli pro krále
ve stáří dvaceti let
vy s kormidlem v ruce
vy běžte a pro nové
dobyjte nový svět.

Kolumbus
Palos, 1492

V Terezíně 1943

2. "I" (a portrait); 3. Reflections on work. I chose the first topic and wrote about insults. Then I tried to finish my geometry homework, but somehow that's not working out. Now I am lying and writing this, because the flickering light has steadied somehow. But now I shall stop and try to sleep, because it's almost half past ten. Cuml and Kalíšek are discussing literature and inversed word order. I finish and go to bed. I'm wondering what my family are doing in Prague. I can hardly remember what Eva looks like any more.

February 9, 1944:

At eight o'clock we had an evening of Chinese Poetry. The speaker was Zdeněk Jelínek. The most important idea in his introduction: People are the same everywhere. Chinese poetry is a people's poetry.

February 16, 1944:

... I herewith declare that writing a diary is stupid, because you put things into it that everyone should keep to himself, and uninvited sons of bitches stick their noses into it.

65

VEDEM, Terezín 1944

The Life of an Inanimate Object

As most of us know, an inanimate object can never, under any circumstances, enjoy life. Only an object in constant contact with people can change, because it is really a part of their lives. Only such an object may be referred to as living. One such object is a curse. "You stupid idiot, you cess pit …" I still remember clearly how Volk's first welcoming speech affected me after the arrival of the DQ transport. It was as though, for a little while, I could feel Prague breathing on me, with her well-lit streets, her silent embankments, and the glittering Vltava river. It was then that I realized there was something to a swearword, that it mirrors its origin the same way national costumes, customs and art do.

There are elegant and vulgar swearwords. Some are civilized, others are what I would almost call prehistoric. We don't have to look far for civilized swearwords. We hear them wherever we go: Idiot, cretin, primitive fool! It may be observed that such curses draw on modern scientific discoveries. On the other hand I once listened to a negro who let off steam in the following way: he rolled his eyes, flared his nostrils and was heard to croak: Bovo, vire capscu! (May you be eaten by an ox!)

I chose these two examples deliberately. Let us look at Terezín swearwords. (I did not make these up, I heard them with my own ears): You f….g primitive oaf, you faded cretin, you materialistic, egoistic swine! Here we may notice two features: one a sign of civilization and the other not unlike that of the negro. The explanation is simple. Terezín is a town where superficial civilization is more

and more suppressed by the instinct for self-preservation, by egoism, the law of the fist, and many more aspects which the outside world has already succeeded in eliminating to a certain degree.

You can know the world through its curses. I dream of hearing the coolies curse in Shanghai and Singapore, the fishermen in Newfoundland, the farmers in Ceylon, the geishas in Japan, the pearl fishers in the Bay of Bengal.

And one day, having learnt about the world and its people through their swearwords, I would return home by steamer across the Pacific. The noise of the ship's screw would lull me and, satisfied, I would fall asleep and in my mind the throbbing of the propeller would scan Homer's verses:
Soundly he slept throughout the night
Sweet dreams his only fetters.

– nz (*Petr Ginz*)

Petr Ginz
(b. 1928, perished).
"To the Station."
Pencil, 285 × 205 mm.
Jewish Museum, Prague,
Inv. No. 129833.

September 1944:

I have read: Schweitzer: *From my Life and Work*; Binko Šimonovič: *The Vinčić Family*; de Vries: *Rembrandt*; Thomas Mann: *Mario and the Magician*; Dickens: *A Christmas Carol*; Daneš: *The Origin and Extinction of the Aborigines of Australia and Oceania*; Milli Dondolo: *An Angel Spoke*; Karel May: *The Son of the Bear Hunters*; Oscar Wilde: *De profundis and Other Stories*.

Terezín 1944

From Petr Ginz's "Plans"

September (probably 1944):

Do linocuts, drawing, shorthand, English. Take a good look at *Vedem*, its standards, and come up with something, but something really worth doing (possibly linocuts...)
(Unfinished...)

From Petr Ginz's "Time Sheets"

June (1944):

I work in lithography. I have made a physical map of Asia and have started a map of the world.

I have read: Otáhalová-Popelová: *Seneca's Letters*; Arbes: *A Mad Job, My Friend the Murderer, Satan*; London: *The Lost Face*; Musil: *Desert and Oasis*; H. G. Wells: *Christina Alberta's Father*; part of Descartes' *Discourse on Method*.

I have learned: Ancient History (Egyptians, Babylonians, Indians, Phoenicians, Israelites, Greeks, Persians, etc.), the geography of Arabia, the Netherlands and of the moon.

I have drawn: Behind the sheep fold and Vrchlabí. I made a survey of zoology, both mentally and on paper. I go to evening lectures on Rembrandt, the Alchemists, etc. I no longer visit the cooks.

That is Petr's "plan" for the last month of his life, followed by the "time sheets" of his activities for September 1944. He did not live to see the end of the month. Transport Ek of September 28, 1944, took him to Auschwitz, where he probably perished in the gas chambers.

Petr Ginz was born on February 1, 1928, in Prague. His parents, both ardent Esperantists, had met at a Congress of Esperantists. Petr's mother was not Jewish and this is why she is still alive today and why Petr's father and sister Eva also survived. Petr was the only member of the family who lost his life. But he lives on in the memory of his nearest and dearest. The scores of boys of the Republic of Shkid and the hundreds of thousands of children who also passed through Terezín have no one to remember them. So let Petr's parents and his sister speak – for Petr and for all those who, like him, remained "one of us."

From the Recollection of Petr's Father, Oto Ginz (Kiryiat Yam, Israel, April 1972)

Before Hitler occupied Czechoslovakia we lived as a small, happy family in Prague. My mother Berta, nee Šťastná (1867), came from Jiřice near Brandýs nad Labem. The rest came from the region of Kouřim: my father Josef, born in 1857 in Barchovice, and his five children, who were born in Ždanice, where father taught at the village school.

The First World War separated us for five years, but at the end of it we met again, more or less in good health.

I am the only one to have survived that terrible tempest unleashed by Hitler. My father died after an illness in 1912 and all the rest perished due to the German intervention.

Those of the next generation of our family must also be counted among the victims: our son Petr and his cousin Pavel (b. 1927), the son of my youngest brother, Miloš.

Eva was taken to Terezín on May 17, 1944, and I myself went on February 11, 1945. We returned together on May 14, 1945. I won't speak of the emotions aroused in us when we reached Prague again. We walked home from Wilson Station: there was no public transport at all.

Our hearts were pounding as we approached our house. Our dear mother was watching for us from the window as she had done for many days. As we embraced, with tears streaming down our faces, Mother cried, "Where is Petr?" She was quite sure that she had seen him with us from the window. How painful it was to tell her that all along the way people had stopped us and asked after him. One of them, a young man, came right to our door with us. We assured

Petr Ginz
(1940 [?] in Prague).
Photograph provided by Petr's sister Mrs Eva Ginzová-Pressburgerová, Beersheva, Israel.

Petr Ginz
(b. 1928, perished).
Illustration to his serial "The Cunning Drews."
Pencil, 145 × 210 mm.
Memorial of Terezín, *Vedem* p. 123.

Petr Ginz with parents and
sister.
Photograph provided by
Petr's father Ota Ginz,
Kiryiat Yam, Israel.
Jewish Museum, Prague,
Neg. No. 29640.

* He's referring to
the improvised lessons
in L 417. "Fifth form"
is an exaggeration
to please his parents.

Mother that many more of the prisoners would return and that we would all meet again.

But the weeks and months passed and our hopes faded. Still, the three of us hoped against hope that we would see Petr again. There were rumors that the Soviet Army had taken a large number of the imprisoned children to the Soviet Union to recuperate. We couldn't stand the uncertainty any longer. I wrote to Michail Sholokhov, with whose family I had spent unforgettable moments. Misha soon wrote back that unfortunately I had been mistaken: no young prisoners had been taken to the Soviet Union after the war. And that put an end to all our hopes.

Near the Letná Fair Grounds there were huge sheds where the children destined for transport to Terezín had to assemble. The Prague Jewish Community had covered the earthen floors with old mattresses. It was to this place that I accompanied Petr one October morning in 1942. Our conversation was serious but I avoided putting sad thoughts into his head. We comforted each other with the thought that we would soon meet again with Mother. Shortly before we parted, I warned Petr what I had learned from acquaintances, that he should be very careful in his contacts with German guards. We walked together up to the point beyond which accompanying persons were not allowed to go. I embraced Petr, we kissed, and he walked away toward the gate. He turned back several times, we waved, and then he disappeared inside the gate. I don't know how I got back home. I knew that my wife's nerves could not have stood the parting I had just gone through.

We wanted to hear as often and as much as possible from each other and so we used every opportunity to let each other know how we were. When the postcards Petr was allowed to send no longer sufficed, he wrote using the name of some friend in Terezín who had no one to write to. This is how we got postcards from him signed by an unfamiliar name. To make matters worse, Petr did not know German very well, so the news he sent was usually pretty basic. Eventually, he found a means to correspond more openly. We don't know how he made friends with some Czech gendarmes on duty in Terezín, but he did. Some of them must have offered to take his letters to Prague. They must have also seen to it that this secretly transmitted news was as innocuous as possible, so they crossed out passages that might have endangered the bearer. In this way we received several long letters from our mother (sometimes heavily censored) and long, rich and detailed uncensored letters from Petr, written in Czech. They are priceless to us, though after all these years they are sometimes difficult to decipher.

We were overjoyed at every bit of news from our loved ones, but we were encouraged as well by every word from friends who were not blood relations. The head of the children's home in which Petr lived referred to our son in one of his letters as "the pride of our home." And in another letter we read, "I can only report the best about Petr. He is a jewel of a boy."

On a thin, transparent strip of paper, sent secretly by Petr, was the following letter, uncensored and undated:

My dear Daddy, Mummy, and Eva

I am still all right, although not quite as well as before. But you needn't worry about me. I hope you've received the parcel voucher. Please send some Haschler cough drops for Grandma (she's got a cough), and for me, some chewing gum, copy books, a spoon, a mess kit, bread and some engravings. Everything here is quite new: the bunks, the names of the streets, the entire administrative apparatus, and that's one reason I'd like to have something old here, something that reminds me of the time when I was with you (when I colored those engravings). The magazine I'm editing is still being published. I write some serious stories for it, and sometimes I even try my hand at philosophizing. Otherwise I attend the fifth form* and my lessons are going well. Next week we're having exams. On the material side of things, every evening I visit Grandma, and she always gives me something to eat. I often get something to sink my teeth into from Uncle as well. Re shoes: next to me on the bunk is a boy who works at the cobbler's. So shoe repairs aren't a concern. Re clothes: I can't

wear the brown pants any more, so I'm wearing the trousers you sent me, and father's quilted jacket. Three weeks ago we had a case of polio in our room. We all got an injection of blood from one of the adults. Rudi Freudenfeld* gave me his blood. Thank God there were no new cases.

Love and kisses from your

Petr

P.S. Send me a book on sociology.

Jméno s uvedením změn   osob | zvířat

Petr Ginz
(b. 1928, perished).
"Terezín."
Pencil, 175 × 250 mm.
Provided by Petr's sister
Eva Ginzová-Pressburgerová,
Beersheva, Israel.
Photograph by Naomi Salmon.

Recollections
from Eva Ginzová-Pressburgerová,
Petr's Sister
(Beersheva, Israel, April 1972)

Like so many girls of my age (I was fifteen) I kept a diary.

On May 15, 1945, I wrote: "Yesterday morning I came home from Terezín. Petr was not there, although I was secretly hoping he would be. We wait every day for him to show up, or at least to send some news of himself. I am finishing my diary with this, because I want to have only my experiences from Terezín in it. But when Petr comes home I shall add that…"

On April 14, 1947, I added one sentence in conclusion: "Petr has not returned."

But it seems to me that this sentence, written two years later, does not belong. The diary has indeed remained unfinished. Because we are still waiting for Petr. It's unbelievable. It seems to me that this gap, this vacuum caused by the senseless slaughter of millions of people, must be filled again. I often think what my life would have been like if Petr had been with me, as he was until I was twelve. Petr was more gifted and stronger than me, and I admired him. He was always my model, he showed me the way. The world would be richer, different, if all those millions of people that are no longer with us had lived. I think human souls are somehow linked to each other. If one of them dies by force, another suffers forever. Something is gone.

I only remember few details of these beautiful years that we spent together. I was only twelve when they dragged him away. I remember our walks together through the streets of Prague, wearing our yellow stars. There were only a few places we were allowed to go. Very often, places we liked to visit – the park, the museums, the library – carried notices saying: No Jews allowed. We carried briefcases under our arms and Petr would tell me when to cover the star with it. One day, when we came to our auntie's shop, we stopped in shock. The NOTICE was there. We went to the outskirts of Prague, as far as Trója bridge. On the way I said that Auntie hadn't meant it for us, she'd probably been forced to put it up: "Jews not welcome" – or perhaps it said "No Jews allowed," I can't remember exactly. Petr was silent. As was usual for children, we ran for a while, then we walked. When we got to the Vltava, he sat down on the riverbank, took out a piece of paper and started to draw. He drew a half-liter glass of beer, a fat face, a dove, and other things I can't remember. And above it all he wrote: "This is the dovelike nature."

When he was twelve or thirteen, at the time of the German occupation, he wrote a novel.** It was the product of a child's imagination. I think he wrote it under the influence of Jules Verne's novels, or at least out of admiration for them. The novel begins when an unpublished and unknown manuscript is found in the cellar of Jules Verne's house. The idea is that this book is now being added to the writer's canon. It's about a group of people in Africa who create a monster, a huge lizard, which they use to try and rule Africa. It was a long novel, full of exciting details in the manner of Jules Verne.

* Rudolf Franěk.
** Petr Ginz's novel *A Visit from Pre-Historic Times* was found and shown at the Exhibition "Art in Terezín 1941–1945," held at the Minor Fort in Terezín, 1972–1973.

Petr Ginz
(b. 1928, perished).
"Terezín."
Pencil, 175 × 250 mm.
Provided by Peter's sister
Eva Ginzová-
Pressburgerová,
Beersheva, Israel.
Photograph by Naomi
Salmon.

I don't know where the manuscript ended up. I don't think it was merely that Petr was broadening and deepening the fantasies stimulated by reading Verne's books. There was more to it. The monster and the imperialism of its creators seemed too much like Hitler. Petr probably thought that Verne, who had imagined and predicted so many seemingly impossible events, couldn't possibly have had the imagination to invent Hitler, so there was a gap here to be filled in. Or perhaps Petr, as a child, wanted to feel that what was happening to him in the world was not real, that it was just part of some fantastic novel.

* Petr's cousin, who was
  one year older.

Terezín 1944

Excerpts from the Terezín Diary of Eva Ginzová, aged fourteen

August 16, 1944:

Petr is an awfully clever boy. When I came here a girl asked me if Petr Ginz was my brother. She said he was supposed to be the most intelligent boy in the "Heim." I was overjoyed and very proud of him.

September 16, 1944:

I have not written anything for a long time; I couldn't get around to it. Petr was ill. He had a temperature of 102. There is such an epidemic now in Terezín. Fevers, but there is no pain. I was worried sick that Peter might have something serious, after all we two are alone here and if something happened to him, how could I answer for it to our parents?

September 27, 1944:

Petr and Pavel* are in the transport. They got their summons the day before yesterday. They were supposed to leave the next day, but they're still here, because the train did not arrive. They live in the attics of the Hamburg barracks…

We all hope that the transport will stay here. There is supposed to be a strike all over the protectorate and this is why the train is not coming. When I learned that Petr was going, I felt sick. I ran away to the washroom, where I cried and cried.

I am trying to be calm in front of Petr. I don't want him to be even more upset. They are supposed to be going somewhere near Dresden, and I am terrified that there will be bombing attacks there and something might happen to the boys. Mummy and Daddy, I miss you awfully, especially now when I am losing the only person who stood by me. Who knows if we all shall meet again? If only the war were over. It is getting to be too much for us! What will they say at home when they find out that Petr has gone? They will soon find out. Karel Müller has written home. Poor Mummy and Daddy.

September 28, 1944:

The train is here and both the boys have got

on already. Petr is Number 2392 and Pavel 2626. They are together in one carriage. Petr is amazingly calm. Uncle Miloš* was full of admiration. I was hoping all the time the train wouldn't come, even though I knew very well it would. But what can you do? This morning Hanka (my cousin) and I went to see them at the Schleuse. It was a terrible sight. I shall never forget it. A crowd of women, children and old men were milling round the barracks to get a last look at their sons, husbands, fathers or brothers. The men hung out of the windows, pushing each other aside to see their loved ones. The whole barracks were surrounded by gendarmes so that nobody could run away. Ghetto guards stood at the building and drove people who had come too close away. The men at the windows waved and said goodbye to their relatives with their eyes. You could hear sobbing everywhere. We ran quickly and brought the boys two slices of bread each, so they wouldn't be hungry. I pushed through the crowd, slipped under the rope that kept people back from the barracks and passed the bread up to Petr at the window. I still had time to shake his hand through the bars, and then the ghetto guards chased me away. I was lucky to get away with it. Now the boys have gone. All that is left are their empty beds.

October 12, 1944:

It is a fortnight today since the boys have left, and there is no news from them. Altogether seven transports left, the summonses for the last were issued yesterday, and some more are supposed to leave.

October 16, 1944:

For the first time after quite a long period there was an air raid warning again today. I saw some foreign planes. First there were a lot and then we saw four, chased by German fighters. I am terribly worried that there will be air raids where our boys are. Who knows if I shall ever see our Petr again? The dear boy! Surely God could not let that happen!

October 28, 1944:

Today is again a sad day! Uncle Miloš joined a transport to the East a little while ago. He got his summons today at about midnight, and had two hours to get ready. Günther** apparently came and was very angry with Rahm*** that there were so many Jews left. It is a month today since the boys left, and now Uncle is going. Hanka and I are left behind all alone, the ones from our family.

November 2, 1944:

Yesterday I found Petr's diary. When I read it I could not help myself and I cried. The poor darling! Miloš's family did him wrong when they said he neglected his parents. You can see from his diary with what great love he remembered his home. I miss them all so much, but I don't show it in front of Hanka. I don't want to worry her. I want to go home!

February 11, 1945:

A transport is due from Prague at six o'clock. I am terribly excited.

February 15, 1945:

Daddy has been here for four days. I can't find any time at all for writing. I think Daddy is hungry. What sort of food is this for a hard working man? I promised I shall try to make Father's life in Terezín easier and I am trying to keep my promise as best I can. He has not found anybody here from the whole family except Hanka and myself. Grandma died before I came and all the others have gone East with the transports.

April 23, 1945:

Dear God, what is happening here, I can't even describe it. One afternoon (Friday, April 20) I was at work, when we saw a freight train passing. People stuck their heads out of the window. They looked simply awful. Pale, completely yellow and green in the face, unshaven, like skeletons, sunken cheeks, their heads shaved, in prisoners' clothes … and their eyes were glittering so strangely … from hunger. I immediately ran into the ghetto (we are working outside) to the station. They were just getting out of the trucks, if you could call what they did getting out. Only a few managed to keep on their feet (their legs were just shanks covered with skin); the rest were lying completely exhausted on the floor of the trucks. They had been on the road for a fortnight and had been given almost nothing to eat. They were coming from Buchenwald and from Auschwitz. They were mostly Hungarians and Poles. I thought I would go mad with excitement, because all the time I was looking for Petr among them. A few of them had left from here, but Petr was not among them. Then one transport after another began to

* Ota Ginz's brother – note E.G.
** Chief of the SS anti-Jewish Center in Prague.
*** Last Commandant of Terezín.
**** Łódź.

arrive. Hungarians, French, Slovaks, Poles (they had been in the concentration camps for seven years) and some Czechs as well. None from our lot. And the corpses among them! A heap in every truck. Clothed in rags, barefoot or in broken clogs. They were taking them away from the concentration camps because the Russians were supposed to be approaching. Such a terrible sight as few can have seen. If only I could express everything on paper. But I haven't enough talent to do it properly. And how these poor creatures threw themselves at any food they got, whatever it was. And how they fought for it – awful! Some of them have paratyphoid and many other terrible diseases. And those who came from Litzmanstadt**** and Birkenau, what they had to tell! Auschwitz and Birkenau are really the same. They were two adjoining camps. All that is now occupied by the Russians. Everyone who arrived by transport in Birkenau was immediately stripped and classified. Children under fourteen and people over fifty went immediately into the gas chambers and then were cremated. They also constantly selected some from those remaining to gas. And the miserable food! Coffee, soup, coffee, etc. I wouldn't have believed it if those who had lived through it hadn't told me themselves. I am so worried about what has become of our Petr. Is he still alive at all?

Petr Ginz
(b. 1928, perished).
„Terezín at Night."
Pencil, 155 x 210 mm.
Provided by Petr's sister
Eva Ginzová-
Pressburgerová,
Beersheva, Israel.
Photograph by Naomi
Salmon.

**Excerpts from the Recollections
of Petr's Mother Miriam Ginzová
(Kiryiat Yam, Israel, April 1972)**

After my marriage I moved to Prague, where my husband's mother and four brothers and sisters lived. Our two children, Petr and Eva, were born there. Every week we went with the children to see mother. She was fond of me, although I did not have a Jewish background. Her daughters sometimes accused her of treating me like a daughter and them like daughters-in-law. I learned a lot from her about how to run a Jewish home.

When Petr reached school age we entered him in the Jewish school in Jáchymova Street, and two years later Eva started there. It was a progressive school with excellent teachers. The language of instruction was Czech. One of the great advantages was the friendly and communal relationship between teachers and pupils. They had considerable freedom and I think each one of them could fully develop his or her talents and abilities.

Petr was well liked by his fellow pupils. I don't remember ever having seen him fighting in front of the school as other boys so often seem to do. His teachers also liked him. When there was some celebration, on feast days or at the end of term, the teachers always gave him a nice part to play which really fit his personality. I remember for instance, how – with a golden crown on his head and a scepter in his hand – he played the part of King Ahasver who drove out his lazy wife Vashti and married a humble Jewish girl, Esther. Esther then interceded with the king and saved all the Jews in the country from being exterminated by the wicked Haman. "I couldn't have given Petr any other part than that of the good man. He wouldn't have been at all suitable for the evil Haman," his teacher said. He was a very sensitive child. When our maid sang a song called "The Orphan Child" he began to weep and begged her not to sing it.

He had a long way to go to school. We lived in Stárkova Street near the Denis Railway Station and to get to school he had to walk along several noisy streets and cross two busy intersections. In the beginning I walked to school with him, but later he went with his fellow pupil Felix Bardach who lived in the next street, Petrská Street. Felix was a small, weak boy. It was only accidentally that I learned Petr always carried Felix's heavy satchel as well as his own.

One of the evacuation transports arriving in Terezín from other concentration camps during the last days before liberation.
Jewish Museum, Prague, Neg. No. 21691.

Petr was a voracious reader. Jules Verne was his favorite, and he also began to write himself. His first efforts were naive children's stories that he illustrated himself. Eva imitated him. She always saw him as her model and she began to write as well.

It's hard to believe just how modest Petr was. Once, just before his birthday – he must have been about ten – we were trying to find out what present he would like. First he insisted that he didn't need anything, then he stopped and said hesitantly that there was something he would like, but that it might not be possible. When I insisted that he tell me, he said he'd love it if I would sew him another pocket into the jacket he wore at home, "but only if it wasn't too difficult."

When we could no longer have a maid – because we were a Jewish family – he constantly offered to help me and whatever I asked he did willingly. That was when both children started to wear the Jewish star… But soon they closed down the Jewish school and there was nowhere for the children to go to school. Petr enjoyed long walks. He used to take public transport outside of Prague as far as the Šárka valley, and whenever possible, he preferred to be alone. What thoughts might he have been thinking on his lonely excursions, into what dream world did he try to escape? We were living in chaos and fear at that time. My husband had lost his job and was washing dishes in the Jewish hospital and I scrounged for food, for the Jewish rations were meager. There wasn't even any milk for the children.

For a while Petr learned to clean typewriters at the Jewish community center and to do small repairs. That kept him busy for some time.

When large groups of Jews started being deported to Terezín, Petr kept an eye out for older and weaker people and helped them carry their luggage as close to the assembly point as possible, though he wasn't particularly strong himself. The Germans strictly forbade others to come to the assembly point, and sometimes they detained such people as well.

In October, 1942, Petr was taken by transport to Terezín. When saying goodbye at home he was brave about it, so as not to make things more difficult for me, and he even consoled me: "Don't cry, Mummy," he said, "and don't worry about me, I'll come back to you."

He was in Terezín for two years, and Eva, who was taken from us in May, 1944, when she turned fourteen, met him there. That's what the Germans did with Jewish children from "mixed marriages."

As long as my children were in Terezín I consoled myself with the thought that they would come back. When I learned from friends – it was in the street in Prague – that Petr had been deported from Terezín, I fainted dead away. I felt that something terrible had happened.

That was only confirmed ten years later. Until then, I was still hoping for a miracle. Jehuda Bacon, who left Terezín on the same transport as Petr, told us that at the Auschwitz station, immediately upon arrival, they sorted the prisoners out into two groups. To the left and to the right. Those to the left went into the gas chambers. And he saw Petr going that way.

You, who are called Merciful, how could you let that happen!

We try not to think about it, not to remember, so that we can go on living at all.

VEDEM, Terezín 1944

Mad Augustus

The air was damp and cold. A tattered steel-gray fog hung just above the waves, almost touching it. Miserable weather. The undulating green mass vanished and merged with the fog at about a hundred yards distance. Augustus sat in the cabin of the *Boniface*. They called him Mad Augustus but the young seaman Peter had faith in him. "He's not mad," he said, "he's just different, a little strange, that's all. He probably knows some great secret that you do not and cannot understand."

"You are slowly getting to be like him. You'll go mad for sure if you keep talking to him," said the other sailors.

"They don't know," Augustus used to say, and his eyes – it seemed to Peter – seemed to be looking down from a great mountain hidden behind clouds. No, Augustus was not mad, certainly not, since he could talk so persuasively. And Peter was fond of him, this madman with the deep eyes, and believed in him. Augustus spoke so strangely. "Nobody else in the whole world talks like that," Peter thought. "Never in my life have I heard the captain, the helmsman, the sailors or the people in port talk so strangely." That was his whole world, he knew no other.

It was night. Everybody was asleep, only on deck you could hear the footfall of the guard dog. Peter was dozing off, his muscles soft and relaxed. His whole body seemed free and light and with his body, his soul relaxed and his senses were dulled by the bluish mist of sleep. He lost consciousness.

Suddenly, like a very weak electric shock, he felt a light touch. With difficulty Peter sat up in his hammock, looked round and saw the figure of mad Augustus bending over him. "Come with me!" he said. Peter roused himself and stretched.

"Come quickly," Augustus's voice prompted. Without a word Peter got up, though it was warm under the blanket and cold outside. He followed Augustus without a sound. They went below. Augustus lit a candle. Its weak light could scarcely drive away the darkness that lurked in every corner, in every crack. They came to a small room in the hold. Mad Augustus entered and Peter followed. The key rattled in the lock and then disappeared in Augustut's pocket. He put the candle down in front of him, sat down on a barrel and put his head in his hands. Peter squatted down because he was cold. Augustus raised his head. His expressive face shone in the candlelight. The reflection flickered in his eyes like small fires. Some time passed. Tiny flies fluttered in circles around the flame. Then Augustus spoke, his voice breaking the dead silence. "Life. What is life? It's like the flame of this candle in which foolish insects singe their wings."

There was silence again, broken only by the spluttering of the flame. "Poor flies. Why do they swarm so eagerly round this flame?" He spoke slowly to himself, as if deep in thought. "It's habit… the drive towards individual existence and… uncertainty…" Again he put his head in his hands and said through his teeth, "They fly fascinated round the flame till it burns them and they fall to the ground, destroyed. Fools! Fools? Habit and uncertainty are too strong, they cannot overcome that. Poor insects!"… They both

Petr Ginz ?
(b. 1928, perished).
Illustration.
Aquarelle, 85 × 85 mm.
Memorial of Terezín,
Vedem, p. 61.

sat in silence. Peter wondered why he was here instead of sleeping safely in his cabin.

"Think about life, my boy," said Augustus. "Look, it's like this flame. Can you see? Can you understand? Out of habit, we circle round it, and we must die. We want to express our 'I' and for that we sacrifice everything!"

He reached out and extinguished the candle. Darkness spread through the room. The insects could be heard flying away, no longer fascinated by the flame. They buzzed a little longer, but soon the sound of their wings died out. They must have flown away through some crack.

"Did you see, did you see?" Augustus's voice said in the dark. "Did you take it all in, boy?" he asked again, as he removed the lid from the powder barrel.

"Once more, Flamarion," the captain's voice could be heard as if coming from far away. He was playing cards.

"Deliverance…" Augustus whispered. He raised his hand and threw a burning match into the powder barrel.

The room lit up with tremendous brightness and in the fire of the explosion, Peter saw the gleam of a Great Fusion.

– nz (*Petr Ginz*)

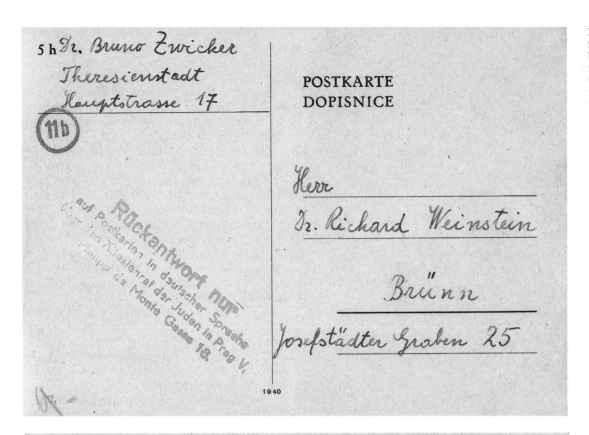

Both sides of a postcard from July 30, 1944, written by Bruno Zwicker. Writing from the ghetto (solely in German) was permitted in rare cases and only on postcards that were strictly censored.
Provided by the authors.

5 h Dr. Bruno Zwicker
Theresienstadt
Hauptstrasse 17
(11b)

Rückantwort nur auf Postkarten in deutscher Sprache über den Ältestenrat der Juden in Prag V, Philipp de Monte Gasse 18.

POSTKARTE
DOPISNICE

Herr
Dr. Richard Weinstein

Brünn

Josefstädter Graben 25

1940

---

30. Juli 1944.

Mein lieber Freund,
beste Grüsse. Hatten große Freude nach so langer Zeit
Deine Karte vom 9. VI. zu lesen. Mit Inhalt u. Deiner
guten Stimmung sehr zufrieden. Ich mit meinen Lieben sowie Valtr und die Seinigen vollkommen gesund. Habe genug Arbeit, studiere in freier Zeit (Spra-
chen), solltest auch etwas von Deinem Arbeitsfach
wiederholen. – Vorige Woche hatte unser Filip eine
Rede über den verstorbenen Direktor Drachmann,
viele Freunde waren anwesend. – Otto's Familie
wohnt seit kurzer Zeit mit Deinem Bruder, wird
Dir schreiben. – Herzlichste Grüsse Deinen Lieben und
allen Freunden.   Dein   Bruno.

78

Bruno Zwicker
(1907–1944).
Provided by the authors.

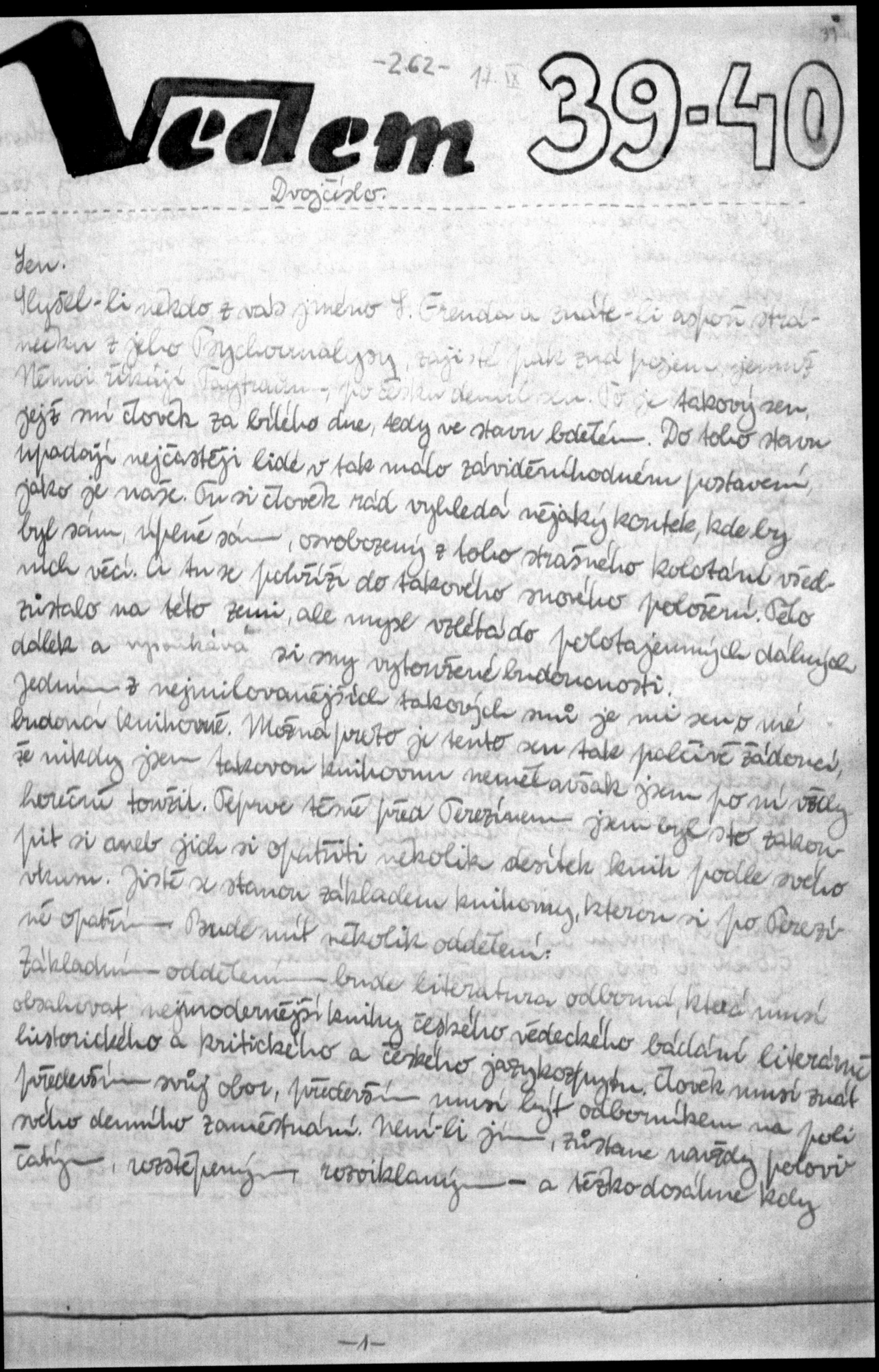
-262- 17. IX

Vedem 39-40

Dvojčíslo.

Sen.

Slyšel-li někdo z vás jméno S. Freuda a znáte-li aspoň stránečku z jeho Psychoanalysy, [illegible] pojem, jemuž Němci říkají Tagtraum, po česku denní sen. To je takový sen, jejž má člověk za bílého dne, tedy ve stavu bdělém. Do toho stavu upadají nejčastěji lidé v tak málo závidění hodném postavení jako je naše. [illegible] si člověk rád vyhledá nějaký koutek, kde by byl sám, úplně sám, osvobozený z toho strašného kolotání všech věcí. [illegible] do takového mořeho položení. Tělo zůstalo na této zemi, ale mysl vzlétá do polotajemných dálných dálek a [illegible] si my vytoužené budoucnosti. Jedním z nejmilovanějších takových snů je mi sen o mé budoucí knihovně. Možná proto je tento sen tak palčivě žádoucí, že nikdy jsem takovou knihovnu neměl, avšak jsem po ní vždy horečně toužil. [illegible]

—1—

Title page, *Vedem*, double number 39–40, September 17, 1943.
Pen, brush, ink, aquarelle, 205 × 279 mm.
Memorial of Terezín, *Vedem* p. 262.

LIFE AND DEATH

VEDEM, Terezín 1943

Life and Death

Life and death, that is the whole world,
A ray of sunlight,
A fiery day,
A violent tempest on the endless sea,
Blood of the living earth – eternal love.

When the trees are in full leaf
When Monday always follows Sunday
When summer breezes list
Through the heart's innumerable pages,
When the sailor young and strong
Fights death in the ocean deep...

Eternally red, life blood
Battles against stone-cold walls,
Ever the world's people
Struggle upwards
Learning to live.

The center is dark. This nothing – this circle –
This nothing is law, space, God.
Next to the whiteness of the clouds,
The poison gas of mocking laughter,
And next to Justice, brown earth,
And then, then bright red love, a dream!

Everything is color: the gray river,
The green fishpond, its nymph,
The yellow rock, the longing
Black circle, the imprisoning universe,
The bright blue sky,
The black and red execution.

Time passed: strangely it twists,
Like a black thread in a constant spiral.
As time goes by, across the ruins
They sing a song of life
Or again, when death strangles them,
They sing the sad song of death.

From the womb of earth life was born
To devour itself, to submit, to fertilize,

Unknown artist
"Death."
Aquarelle, 145 × 210 mm.
Provided by Eva Ginzová-
Pressburgerová,
Beersheva, Israel.
Photograph by Naomi
Salmon.

Once a cell looked round
To live and die.
Life conquered space
To live and become God.

That was man. And man became the
master
Over life and death, his loins, his
shoulders.
Time passes and time twists constantly,
Strangely in a circle, in a spiral.

Today death holds his filthy hand
Over the world and over my soul
But the cup, fashioned of skulls,
With brains shriveled and dried,
Will overflow, and all
The bones, the blood, the muscles call:
"Life! Life! Life!?"

Time presses forward,
The spiral turns,
People are born and die,
History happens, and seems to happen,
At the end of the chain of time
Freed from fetters, from money,
At the end of its wild spiral
Love twists into eternity.

– Ha- (*Hanuš Hachenburg*)

Eva Heská
(b. 1932, perished).
"Heads."
Pastel, 295 × 220 mm.
Jewish Museum, Prague,
Inv. No. 129.

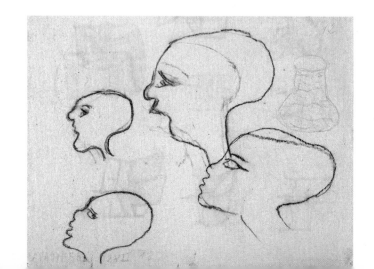

Beno Kaufmann
(b. 1929, perished)
and **Zdeněk Taussig**
(b. 1929, survived).
"Section of the furnace":
illustration to their
commentary "Something
About the Crematorium
and Cremation."
Pen, brush, aquarelle,
200 × 142 mm.
Memorial of Terezín,
Vedem p. 66.

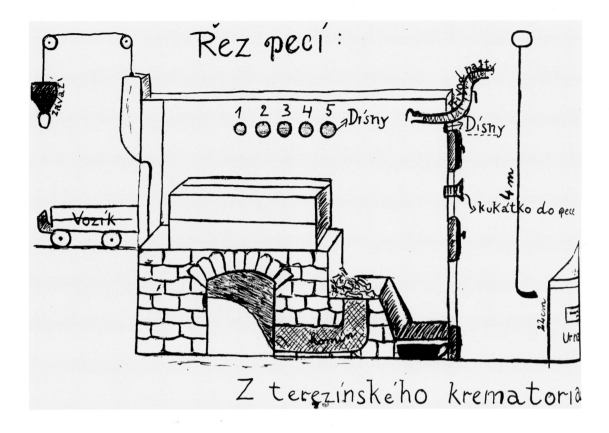

By the end of April 1945, 33,430 prisoners had died in Terezín. Most of the victims were burned in the Terezín crematorium, which was in operation from October 1942 onwards.

VEDEM, Terezín 1943

Something about the Crematorium and Cremation

Many of you surely ask yourselves the question: What is cremation and what does a crematorium look like? First, something about cremation.

From the modern viewpoint cremation is in every respect more hygienic than burial. "Why?" you ask. In the grave flesh decomposes and disappears completely over the course of ten years. Only bones remain.

In cremation, the flesh is consumed within a few minutes. The most interesting part of the crematorium is the furnace, which is heated to a temperature of 800–1200 degrees centigrade. The best furnaces use oil. Six to nine liters of oil are needed to bring the furnace up to temperature. To prevent the temperature from rising above 1200 degrees, cold air is pumped into it through ten small nozzles. Should the temperature drop below 800 °C the nozzles are closed and the temperature rises again. The furnace is lined with fire clay ten centimeters thick.

The procedure during cremation is as follows: the corpse is laid on a heavy iron trolley located at the back on a raised platform, then it is pushed into the furnace through the back door. Here the cart automatically empties its load and returns. The action takes a few seconds. It is well known that the body consists of 75 percent water and therefore, when exposed to great heat, the water in the body begins to boil, which causes the corpse to move. When all the flesh has burned and only a small pile of half-consumed bones remains, the attendant pushes it with the aid of a four-meter-long poker to the central part of the furnace where the bones continue to burn. A second corpse is then put into the furnace above it, so that two are burnt at the same time.

When the bones have been reduced to ashes the attendant pushes them to the lowest section, the grate. Below the grate there is a hopper, where the remnants are sifted and left to cool. A corpse takes between twenty-five and forty minutes to burn completely. It is interesting to note that the cremation time for a woman is only half that of a man.

You will want to know, I'm sure, how the corpses are burnt here in the Terezín crematorium and what the installation is like. The crematorium here in Terezín was established half a year ago, making it the newest crematorium in the protectorate. The bodies of those who have died from infectious diseases or are full of lice are burned in their coffins. The ashes are then put in a paper urn, 22 × 18 cm and placed in the "columbarium" in the former brewery. But I shall tell you about that next time.

– Lightning (*Beno Kaufmann and Zdeněk Taussig*)

This commentary, which was well received by the members of Shkid and other participants of the Friday reading sessions, gave rise to a regular column in *Vedem* called "Rambles Through Terezín." The actual instigator was Petr Ginz who, along with Beno Kaufmann, was one of the most frequent contributors to the feature.

Central morgue
of the Terezín Ghetto.
Photograph
by Vlasta Gronská, 1972.

VEDEM, Terezín, 1943

Rambles Through Terezín

The *Zentralleichenkammer**** is situated at the very edge of Terezín. It lies deep within the fortifications. The entrance looks like the gates of Hell. Only a dim light penetrates from the outside through the embrasures. Every now and then a cart rumbles up laden with corpses and behind white-coated pallbearers. Their steps echo through the underground passages. Coffins made of planks are stacked in dead-end tunnels. Some are full and ready to be taken away, some are empty, waiting for their lodgers.

This was the scene that met my eyes when I visited this gloomy place. Silence reigned, even the attendants working at the back in the corridors talked in whispers. The oppressive terror of death lay over everything. When I got to the end of the passage, the attendants were just wrapping a corpse. That was a terrible sight, because the outlines were so clear, yet the figure was immobile and stiff. When they had finished wrapping the corpse they laid it in the coffin and covered it with the lid. A rabbi was attending. I watched for a while and then asked for further information from Dr. Bock, the manager of this ghetto terminus.

"The *Zentralleichenkammer* has been here since August 12, 1942, and by now 21,000 corpses have passed through its corridors."

* Central Mortuary.

Crematorium in the Jewish Cemetery. Memorial of Terezín, Inv. No. A 780.

Cart with corpses in front of the crematorium. Memorial of Terezín, Inv. No. A. 782.

Burial in mass graves. Memorial of Terezín, Inv. No. A 785.

Mass graves near the crematorium. Memorial of Terezín, Inv. No. A 764.

"How many of those died of infectious diseases?" I asked.

"We don't keep records of that. I only know that 120 died of typhoid."

"What happens to the deceased? What's the procedure?"

"They usually die in the infirmary. After the post-mortem examination by the doctor, the corpse is immediately brought here, where it is washed in keeping with religious observances, dressed in a shroud and placed in a coffin. Everything is done under the supervision of the rabbis. After cremation, the remains are placed in urns, for which a columbarium is being established in the casemates."

"What about the feelings of the attendants who constantly work with corpses? Do they handle them like bricks or treat them like dead human beings?"

"It is the only job where there can be no thought of reward. They take their work seriously and carry out this final service to the dead conscientiously. That was clear last September, when they had to deal with 4,000 corpses at once. Even then they did not fail. It wasn't physical strength that kept them on their feet, it was something more."

"Many thanks, Doctor Bock, for your information. I won't keep you any longer." After saying my farewells, I returned from the bowels of the earth into the brightness of a sunny September day.

– nz (*Petr Ginz*)

87

A stirring event in the life of the prisoners of Terezín was the "census" held on November 11, 1943, in the valley of Bohušovice.

___

VEDEM, Terezín 1944

Sensation – the oddest event
of the twentieth century!
– Nothing – just
a slight derailment
and on we go

It was last November 11 [1943]. Several persons were rumored to have disappeared from the ghetto and the "higher ups" wanted to make sure. [...] Early that morning thousands of people were lined up in huge ranks in front of their lodgings. Old people, young people, even babies in their prams. It was cold that day and there was very little food. We waited for the order and then we set out, winding and twisting like a huge, endless snake. There were the weak and infirm, old men and women who no longer looked like normal human beings their age, exhausted by early rising and by this whole life, circling round them like a nebulous sphere of hope. For a time the stream of people became straighter with the arrival of men and women who were a little stronger and had some endurance. But they, too, were apathetic and resigned to the life they led. Then came a herd of scampering children, full of pranks, treating the spectacle around them as a huge joke, which in a way was the most sensible attitude of all. Last but not least came the babies in their prams, sound asleep and unaware of their surroundings.

After a march of four hours, we had all arrived at our destination and now stood waiting obediently and at attention, to see what they would do to us. They walked up and down among us with their sticks, careful not to get dirty or dusty, and often they would kick us. We stood there, numb with cold, starving and exhausted, for a full twelve hours. We could hear the sick calling out, the small children crying. Old people fainted and we shifted from one foot to the other uncertainly. "What will they do with us next?" someone asked. Nothing. No one knew anything. It was already getting dark and we were still standing there waiting for salvation, like slaves begging their masters not to whip them. How many faithful lost faith in their God that day, a God in whom they had until so recently believed? We thought that this time, they would leave us here to die of hunger and cold. There were 30,000 of us and only a few of them, yet there was nothing we could do in our impotence. It was not enough to call out, "Hurrah, up and at them!" as one would in a revolution. We had no weapons and they would have gunned us down. We were all very weak as well. How many chances were there to escape from the ghetto, and yet no one dared? Suddenly, we all wanted to be "home" again in the ghetto.

By seven o'clock it was pitch dark. There was confused movement in the crowd. Everyone was searching for familiar faces in the dark to ask what all this was about and to complain. Some were crying, some were laughing. I wept in anger. I was too fond of life to sacrifice it to these scoundrels. The things I realized then! Most of all I thought about my past and my shattered future. I still had many plans. How wonderful it would be, I thought, if I could carry them out. The people who were laughing had forced themselves to laugh, perhaps to forget their pitiful present.

And suddenly it started. A great wave, as if a rope had been loosened and everything was bursting loose. We surged forward. No one knew who had given the command, but on we went, like a slow avalanche, killing everything in its path. A crush. You could hear shouts. People trampled under foot, everyone thinking only of himself. Me! Nobody else counts! It was a matter of life and death. We surged up to the buildings that stood in our way. The crowd was pressed into a solid mass. It was impossible to breathe. Everyone stood still. Then we were swept on again, almost unaware of ourselves. The strength of the individual counted for nothing. Cordons of men trying to keep order were pushed aside. Only one terrifying force existed, the force of the whole, irresistible and cruel.

Yes, and yet we managed to get home. Nobody knew exactly how. Everybody ran for his life, leaving everything behind. We escaped like flies from the spider's web with terror in our faces, though we were used to such things. It was soon forgotten.

Life goes on.

It was November 11. Is there more to come?

... Echo.

– Z. Orče (*Zdeněk Ornest*)

The first transports to Terezín and leaving from there "to the East" were received at and dispatched from the Bohušovice railway station. Later on the prisoners of Terezín had to build a spur from Bohušovice to Terezín.

VEDEM, Terezín 1943

The First Train

It stopped at the wooden barrier, whistling woefully.
It can't have wanted to go on,
To a place beyond the grave,
And destroy the colors painted on its body.

Step by step, it covered the new track.
Three children with large wondering eyes
Watched as the wheels turned
And the train drove down the street.

I closed my eyes. So this is what an unbeating heart
Of steel, driven by steam, looks like.
It gives the world no choice at all
Under your wheels, my dear, I go a little further.

And worms turn green on the iron tracks
They groan, because they're made of muscle,
And whisper aloud their song of love,
You monster, I'm alive. I too am alive.

– Academy* (*Hanuš Hachenburg*)

VEDEM, Terezín 1944

The Hearse

With calm, steady steps the mourners would walk behind the black cart. On it a father, an uncle, or simply an old man in a wooden or metal coffin, depending on the fee paid – for a first, second, or third class funeral. It could be with Chopin's funeral march, for important persons, or with nothing but the mournful howl of a poor unknown dog, the deceased's only friend. That was how the last respects, these final leave-takings of our departed ones were conducted. Flowers, wreaths, black sashes with messages written on them. There were large, medium and small carts, and we turned our backs superstitiously when we met them somewhere on the road. These carts were symbols of death to us, those huge, lumbering coffins, filling us with terror and dismay. We were afraid to touch them. They were not of this world. They belonged to another, distant unknown world.

Months and years have gone by. Again people walk behind these same funeral carts loaded with wood, coal, luggage, furniture – inanimate objects that have never been alive, and therefore have never departed from this world.

A strange feeling came over us when we first saw this image of ghetto life. It stopped us short and confused us. The symbol of another world, the terror of black wood, the last resting place for so many millions – and suddenly they were being used in the public service, for daily work, because there was a shortage of other means of transport.

And the faces of the men walking behind these carts? In the beginning they were sad and serious. "That is our fate, that is our lot, hunted and eternally wandering." But the faces got used to it, and not only that, they even began to smile, and after a time they completely forgot that the cart now laden with milk cans once served a different purpose.

We have shown once more that we will not let our heads hang, that we are able to overcome even such ignominy. With our heads held high and proud. Beat us, shame us, make life impossible for us, we shall overcome, for even death has lost its secret terror for us, and the funeral cart – this currus moratorium – "Hey, Frank. Bet you I can drive this jalopy through the gate without crashing it!"

– ele (*probably Josef Stiassny*)

The Thaw

Silently, lightly, slowly it drifts down
Onto the black and bleeding earth,
From somewhere up high, steadily descending
Whirling in the air on a tender breeze.

Covering all and glittering strangely,
As if to envelop this aged rot
And as in a dream, suddenly everything
Becomes once again what it once used to be.

Hidden is the filth that blankets the world
Hidden the darkness that blinds us all
Hidden the hunger that makes us retch,
Hidden the pain that breaks our backs.

Just for a while we breathe again freely
Drugged by the glitter, by the world all in white
I look out the window, the steady snow falling
And suddenly everything's water again.

– Orče (*Zdeněk Ornest*)

The Physician
and Terezín

One of the most dedicated workers in Terezín is he who battles with death – the Physician. The doctor of Terezín surely has a task more responsible than any other doctor in the world. Day after day his hands touch people, whether during the many operations he must perform, at a delivery, or during a blood transfusion. Naturally the doctor's work has been made easier since many essential medical aids have arrived in the ghetto, such as injections, equipment for the operating theater, etc. But what was it like, say, two years ago?

I used to know one of the physicians (presently in Poland), Dr. F. Mladý, a man of great temperament, strong, ambitious, with about four years of practice behind him. He came with four hundred other men in the AK transport. One day one of the men who were sharing a room with him complained of sharp pains on the right side of his abdomen. The doctor waited a day and because the pain did not let up, he diagnosed appendicitis. But how was he to operate? There was no operating room, no reliable sterilizing medium, no recovery room. But he convinced himself the operation would work, and next morning he proceeded. Three days and three nights the patient hovered between life and death, tossing and turning with a high fever. For three days the doctor did not leave his bedside (it hardly deserved this name), nursing his patient as if he were his own child. He scarcely ate, washed, or slept. On the fourth day the crisis was over and the patient, who would surely have died without the dedicated care of Dr. Mladý, slowly recovered.

Like him, the majority of doctors in Terezín, even without essential materials, fought death without the slightest financial advantage to themselves.

– Don Herberto (*Herbert Fischl*)

Petr Jellinek
(b. 1931, perished).
"The Square in Terezín."
Pencil, 265 × 210 mm.
Jewish Museum, Prague,
Inv. No. 130744.

One of the everyday aspects of life in the Terezín Ghetto

It is cold. The streets of Terezín are completely snowed under and the snow is already beginning to freeze in the bitter cold. I amble slowly along the sidewalk, watching life in the street. Suddenly I catch sight of an old man of about eighty, with white hair and a white beard. Were I to judge him by the way he walks I wouldn't put him at more than forty. He walks briskly, carrying his mess kit. Perhaps he is going to fetch his lunch. Suddenly he stumbles and falls on the frozen, unsanded sidewalk. He hits his head on the pavement and lies there without moving. Passersby rush up to help the old man and one of them, a doctor, judging by the badge of Aesculapius he is wearing, examines the old man, but all he can do is confirm death.

A few days after this occurrence I visited one of the blocks. As I entered one of the many rooms, a terrible stench hit me. Along the dusty walls there were two rows of wooden bunks. When I went further into the room I saw that the bunks were occupied by many old men and women with sunken cheeks. Some were groaning weakly. I ap-

proached a man in a white coat who was on duty with two nurses. I asked what the matter with these people was, and where in fact I was.

"My boy," said the man in the white coat, "this is the hospital for the aged. Most of them are suffering from pneumonia. Don't forget, we're in Terezín. They get cold in the unheated rooms and crawl into bed for warmth. Then they get pneumonia and in a few days they're gone." And the doctor hurried off.

I am not particularly sensitive but later, when I thought about these two occurrences, which are surely quite common in the ghetto, I felt like crying. Never before had the horror of Terezín struck me so compellingly as then. And once again, I was richer by another experience.

– Don Herberto (*Herbert Fischl*)

Remembrance

In that gray house, an old woman
Suffered on her bed. No one knew her.
And as she shriveled away, with God her only succor
She secretly hugged something to her.

A kind of cardboard box, and when she dies
The ghetto will be her only heir.
And how she cried, that helpless woman.
She wanted to live to see her children one more time.

She did not want to die;
She wrung her hands (or clung to her faded souvenir)
Then in the night, dry for lack of water, died.
I was upset for fully half a day.

When they came for her things in the morning –
Such a beautiful balmy day –
All they found was four simple flowers
And a picture of her son clasped
Tightly in her twisted, stiffened hands.
They took it from her, clumsily, roughly,
And tore it up.

I look at her.
I learned nothing more. But I believe –
                    I hope,
That mother and son were burned together.

– Ha- (*Hanuš Hachenburg*)

Liliana Franklová
(b. 1931, perished).
Aquarelle, pastel,
340 × 215 mm.
Jewish Museum, Prague,
Inv. No. 129378.

Rambles Through Terezín

As you can see, we have introduced a new column. About Terezín. You probably all think that you know Terezín well. With this column I want to prove you wrong.

The De-Lousing Station

One day, when I had nothing better to do, I went for a walk through Terezín with my guide. We splashed aimlessly through the mud of the outskirts of Terezín when suddenly we saw an open gate: the de-lousing station. Our curiosity aroused, we went inside. The first thing we saw was several workers taking lice infested mattresses into the gas chamber. We turned to Doctor Antscherl, who willingly explained everything to us.

"Here," he said, "the mattresses are loaded up and taken to that gas chamber." We looked; one was open and one closed. One was just being filled, in the other the mattresses were being disinfected with Ventox.

"The mattresses," said Dr. Antscherl, "are left in this chamber for five hours at a temperature of 20 degrees C or twelve hours at a temperature of 5 degrees C. To maintain the temperature we have stoves that can be fired from the outside. Each chamber is about fifty to eighty cubic meters in volume. The gas is let in through special vents in the door. All other openings are carefully sealed to prevent the gas from escaping."

"And what is this room for?"

"That is where we store the infested mattresses. I don't advise you to go in there."

"And what are those buildings at the back for?"

"That's the boiler room. A local central heating system is being installed there." Since anything technical interests me, I thanked Dr. Antscherl and went to the next building with my guide.

In the office we got hold of Mr. Porges, the engineer, and asked him to take us round and show us everything. We were not refused here either. He took us to the adjoining room. "This is the boiler room," he said. "Here we make the boilers, the pressure reduction valves and the equipment to settle the salt in the water. We shall have to add blasting ventilators to that equipment standing at the back to speed up the burning of the fuel. The fuel will be coal dust, so heating won't be expensive. Three pipes will come out of the boiler, insulated by molded silicon blocks. One will lead to the Magdeburg kitchen, which is just being set up. The second will go into the next building, to a modern disinfection system and to the baths, which are also nearly finished. And the third will lead to the Kavalír barracks."

"I have to make all the parts myself," Mr. Porges proudly continued, "and I often have to help with the construction as well. Everything should be ready by March 1, and I hope it will." We thanked the engineer and after successfully crossing the lake of mud in front of the building we returned home.

– nz (*Petr Ginz*)

The well-known Czech writer **Karel Poláček** (born March 22, 1892) arrived in Terezín on July 5, 1943, by Transport De, as No. 541. In Terezín he liked the company of young people. For the boys in L 417, and for others as well, he prepared a number of lectures on subjects like the first Czechoslovak president Masaryk and the "Friday Circle" (every Friday Czech intellectuals met with the well-known writer Karel Čapek), Russian realism, and many others.

A "serialized story" started to appear in *Vedem* in response to Poláček's novel, *Men Offside*. Poláček's characters are transposed from the Czech petit bourgeois milieu into the Terezín ghetto. Later they end up in a "Polish" transport. Here are the first two of these stories.

Transport Es left Terezín for Poland on October 19, 1944, and with it Karel Poláček. He never returned.

VEDEM, Terezín 1943

Men Offside
Go to Terezín

A silent night descended over Prague. The coffeehouses and nightclubs filled up. Decent people went home to the bosom of their families.

Mr. Načeradec sighed as he laid down his cards and drew his watch from the little pocket on his considerable stomach. He was shocked to realize that it was going on ten o'clock. He thanked Mrs. Damenstein, said goodbye to her husband and trotted down the stairs to the floor below where he lived with his better half, Hedwig. When he got to the door of his flat he rummaged in his pocket for the keys, but couldn't find them. Then he remembered, with a shock, that he'd left them at home at lunchtime. Somewhat shaken, he pressed the bell. Inside the flat he could hear a rattling noise and finally, after an awful series of animal groans and cursing, the door opened slowly to reveal the aggressive face and broad figure of Mrs. Načeradec, poker in hand. When she saw Mr. Načeradec, she heaved a sigh of relief. "Richard,

95

Unknown artist
Illustration to the serial
"Men Offside."
Crayons, pencil, brush,
aquarelle, 205 × 300 mm.
Memorial of Terezín,
Vedem p. 63.

Unknown artist
Illustration to the serial
"Men Offside."
Pencil, aquarelle,
200 × 296 mm.
Memorial of Terezín,
Vedem p. 69.

darling," she said, "I thought it was a burglar."

Mr. Načeradec, happy at the situation that had developed, because he would not be scolded for being late, pulled his wife back into the flat saying: "But Hedwig, me a burglar? What were you thinking of? I was only having a little game of cards with Mr. Damenstein."

"Oh, Richard, cards, football. I'm so unhappy. If you only knew what sort of a dream I had, what terrible foreboding. Richard, something awful is going to happen today."

But Mr. Načeradec was no longer listening. While his wife kept talking, he undressed, got into bed and soon his peaceful snores filled the room. When Mrs. Načeradec realized he was asleep, she heaved a sigh as if to say she might have made a better match, then she lay down beside her husband. It seemed that nothing would disturb their sleep.

Suddenly hurried steps echoed in the hallway and the bell rang. Husband and wife slept peacefully on. The bell rang a second time, a third time, louder and more urgently. Mrs. Načeradec woke up with a start. The thought flashed through her head: A BURGLAR! She shook her husband awake and with the words: "Richard, protect me!" she threw on her checkered dressing gown and hurried to the door.

With the courage of an Amazon she flung open the door and thrust herself bravely forward. But she started back as if struck by lightning when she heard the words: "*Jüdische Kultusgemeinde,** transport call-up, sign here please." She heard no more. One word only escaped her lips: "Richard…" and then, like a felled tree, she sank to the floor.

Men Offside in Terezín

There was great excitement at the railway station of Terezín. A new transport was due to arrive. The impatient *Hundertschaft*** swore bad-temperedly and sweated. Their all-powerful leader, Petschau, though he was expecting a famous great-aunt to arrive with full rucksacks and cases, was in a bad temper. Suddenly a hooting could be heard and soon the wheezing locomotive appeared, pulling

* Jewish Religious Community.
** *Transporthundertschaft:* a group of workers helping as porters.

96

Unknown artist
Illustration to the serial
"Men Offside."
Pencil, aquarelle,
207 × 300 mm.
Memorial of Terezín,
Vedem p. 84.

* Auxiliary service.
** AK –
Arbeitskommando:
the name given to
the first transports to
Terezín. They were
made up of young
Jews who erected
various camp
installations in the
town. In the
beginning members
of the AK transports
were exempt from
being sent "to the
east" and also
granted certain
privileges that soon
became the target of
criticism and cabaret
jokes.
*** What she really
meant was
Ostentransporte –
which went to
Auschwitz.
**** Porter.
***** Fall in for cleaning
duty.

scenes for he interrupted their joyful out-pouring of feelings: "Move along, move along, ladies."

Just then a young man hurried up and politely relieved Mrs. Načeradec of her luggage. "That must be an AK,"** whispered Mrs. Načeradec gratefully to her friend.

As the kilometer long procession approached Terezín, everybody's mood worsened. Mrs. Načeradec alone happily twittered on. "My dear Clothilde, is it true that some sort of transport, some *Westentransporte*** or something like that are leaving here?"

"Yes, dear Hedwig, it's a terrible thing."

With these words Mrs. Načeradec's mood finally sank to zero. "All of this transport will go to Poland?"

"Oh, no, Hedwig, my dear, the young girls who have a fiance in the AK are bound to stay behind. You know how it is, women and favoritism."

Black night descended upon Mrs. Načeradec's little soul. But a spark of hope lit up her thoughts when she remembered the dashing young man that had carried her suitcase, and her own words: That must be an AK.

At this moment they reached the gate. They walked on and there was no more time to talk. Now Mrs. Načeradec remembered her luggage. She wrung her hands and from her mighty bosom came the cry: "My luggage, we are beggared, we have nothing left at all!" She fainted – straight into the arms of the young *Kofferträger***** who was just bringing her luggage.

Now some more shouting could be heard in the courtyard. "Richard Načeradec, Number 996, *Antreten zur Putzkolonne.*"***** By that time Mr. Načeradec had become so apathetic he scarcely noticed what was going on around him, and fell in without a word. Meanwhile Mrs. Načeradec had come round. The charming porter led her to her bunk and sat down beside her, feeling quite embarrassed.

– CA – KR (*Unknown authors*)

heavily laden carriages. Everybody at the station started to run hither and thither in confusion, shouting contradictory orders that nobody listened to anyway. To make matters worse, a constable of sorts appeared who, when he heard the noise, thought: "I should be put to shame by those Jews?" and began to shout as well. All this was interrupted by the arrival of the train. The brakes grated and streams of Jews poured out.

Mr. Načeradec and the children took hold of their luggage, but Mrs. Načeradec somehow lagged behind. At last she noticed a plumpish woman with the *Hilfsdienst** armband on and ran up to her. The two women embraced and Mrs. Načeradec just managed to get out one word, "Clothilde…"

The constable evidently disliked such

Recollections of Kurt Kotouč, Chairman of the Self-government of Shkid

The pages of *Vedem* will speak to us more intimately, if we understand the intellectual and spiritual world of its authors, which was formed long before they came to Terezín. It was a world of perverted dimensions and precocious maturity, where some features of the child's personality developed quickly, while others remained submerged. The social isolation and the abuse of the Jews' human dignity impinged profoundly on the consciousness of adolescents. My own childhood can throw some light on the experiences common to thousands of children from Jewish families in the two or three years before the war.

I would locate our family somewhere in the lower ranks of the urban middle class. Father, Otto Kotouč (1895–1942), who had been lucky enough to survive the front lines of the First World War, was a textile technician. He himself was the son of a miner from the Oslavany coal mining region. In 1921, still a bachelor, he attempted to become independent by establishing – I quote from the surviving permit – "a business with old and new woven and woolen remnants." This unusual business was to provide a livelihood as well for Father's widowed mother and his sister. In the warehouse near Cejl

Street in Brno, textile remnants were gathered, which the two women then picked apart and sorted. Later on my mother became a "partner" in the business, looking after the paperwork for Father. How unstable this business was is illustrated by the fact that Father's Hadernhandlung (rag business), as the Nazi liquidation order disparagingly but aptly labeled it, was not in business at all between the spring of 1922 and January, 1925.

Father got married in December, 1923. If I consider the good things included in the term "a Czech Jewish family," I see in my mind's eye the Senský family from Mohelno, where my beautiful mother Stella (1902–1942) came from. The Senský family, recognized by the Nazis, in one of its branches at least, as "Aryan," still exists in the Moravian village of Mohelno. Mother's father, Alois Senský, owned a cottage there, now long since demolished, and a general store. The Senskýs were well-liked for their honesty and erudition. Local annals record that they were also elected to the local council, the school board, and even served as mayors. Mother had four siblings who were all well brought up and received what, for those times, was an excellent education. One of them even went to the university. I spent most of my vacations in Mohelno, and was enchanted by the lovely countryside, the dense forests, and the romantic valleys of the Jihlava and Oslava rivers.

In Brno we lived in an old apartment house in Falkensteiner Street. By present-day standards it was a poor environment, a dark flat where you had to bathe in a washtub, but we children were happy there. There was a small garden that went with the flat and our world was the neighborhood around the old Brno brickworks, ruled over by the children of the Brno riff-raff, the thickly overgrown Špilberk, the "Obilňák" or Market place, and on Sunday the Komín district, where we could swim in the Svratka river.

I did not know much about my Jewish origins. My parents belonged to a generation that was rather ambivalent about religion, although Mother had learned to write in Hebrew. Perhaps once a year some member of the family took me to the synagogue or to the Jewish cemetery. None of my close friends were Jews.

In 1939 I was finishing secondary school. Brno, with its large German minority, was suddenly full of dirndls and members of the Henlein organization. And the way to school along the slope of Špilberk Hill had suddenly become dangerous. Members of the Hitler Youth would lie in wait for us and the only permissible defense was to run away. It would have been nothing more than an adventure, if we Jewish children had not been singled out and could have shared these encounters with our other friends as our common fate.

I went to see a school fellow. His mother opened the door a tiny crack. "He's not at home!" The same thing happened again next day, and it was only then that my feelings told me my friend was pretending not to be at home because I was Jewish. I returned home so ashamed that I didn't tell anyone about it, not even my parents.

I met my favorite teacher in the street. He used to praise my brother Hanuš and me for our progress in school. He was now wearing the badge of the National Confederation. He said, "I knew it couldn't turn out any other way for those Jews."

A gang of youths waylaid me near Mohelno. They twisted my arm behind my back and one of them asked, "Do you know where you belong, Jew?"

Somebody happened by, and I was let go. At home my father warned me: "You mustn't go there any more ..." And I realized bitterly that my father could do nothing to help me.

Even against the background of the apocalypse that soon caught up with us, these experiences remained forever engraved on my mind.

We had to give up our buddies and form new friendships with Jewish boys, but there was always an element of self-preservation in these friendships. We exchanged natural relationships for the solidarity of the damned.

In the school year of 1940–1941, I was to begin my studies at the grammar school on Poříčí Street but instead I had to attend the former Jewish grammar school, which no longer had the status of a state school and later even lost its building. To that point the grammar school had been the last refuge for Jewish teachers from all over the country. This is where the future founder of the Terezín Shkid, Valtr Eisinger, met the sociologist, Dr. Bruno Zwicker. Eisinger had taught at the grammar schools in Kyjov and Orlová, and Zwicker was a former lecturer at the faculty of arts at Masaryk University in Brno. In Brno I knew only Eisinger, who taught German to us boys in the third form.

In late 1940, the Gestapo broke into our flat for the first time. Two men dumped the contents of all the wardrobes into the middle of the room. Mother had to pack some of the things, like underwear and pullovers, into cases that were then sealed. A man with a vulgar face declared: "Das wird alles für die NSDAP gut sein! Wir sind nicht eure republikanische Polizei!" (That will all be very useful for our Nazi party. We are not your republican police.) The following day Father had to take the cases to the Faculty of Law, which was now the headquarters of the Brno Gestapo. After two anxious days, Father returned. He even brought the confiscated things back with him. He'd been lucky: the investigating clerk of the Gestapo had once served with him at the front during the First World War and had let him go home.

In 1941 we and two other Jewish families were forced to move into a three-room flat in a large apartment block near Brno-Koliště. I can still see the colorful kaleidoscope of people in that flat crammed together in a small space that had been further reduced in size by an assortment of useless objects from which the owners could not bear to be parted. It was a grotesquely incongruous group. People literally tripped over each other in this blacked-out, Kafkaesque environment as they tried to preserve some dignity by maintaining some superficial conventions.

This flat was also invaded by the Gestapo, in August 1941. In a panic I threw out of the window some butter that my parents had, with great difficulty, managed to scrounge. We lived in the room furthest back, and in the beginning we could only hear the voices of the Gestapo men, but then a scene that I was familiar with from Falkensteiner Street repeated itself. During this raid both my parents and the Weinstein family, who were emigrants from Vienna, were summoned to Gestapo headquarters. The Weinsteins later returned, but made no mention what had happened there. My parents were imprisoned – my father in the Kounic students' residence and my mother in the prison on Cejl Street.

By an odd chance occurrence we managed to see Father several times more, for just a moment. Once a week clean underwear could be brought to the Kounic students' residence and my brother saw Father at the prison window. After that we tried to walk by the residence regularly at the same time, and several times Father indeed looked cautiously out of that window. But soon afterwards my parents were deported to the concentration camps: Mother to Ravensbrück and then to Auschwitz, Father to Auschwitz, where they both died in 1942.

After our parents' imprisonment my brother

and I were left alone in Brno. Only Father's eighty-year-old mother Johanna and his sister Marie were still living there. They were utterly helpless and in 1942 they both died in the Nazi extermination camps of Treblinka and Os-trówo. The first transports were already leaving Brno for Terezín when we were given permission to move to Mohelno and live with Grand-mother and Auntie. We eventually joined a transport with them. I was looking forward to leaving the terrible atmosphere in Brno behind, but it was not much better in Mohelno. We hardly went outside – in the village the uniqueness of our fate seemed even more phantasmagoric, the yellow star on our clothes even more ignominious. We were put into transport Aw departing from Třebíč. A family friend – Rudolf Mohelský, a farmer – took his team of horses and drove my grandmother, my aunt, my brother, and me, and our fifty kilograms of luggage per person, to Třebíč. It was a lovely spring day and as we passed through the villages people stared at his strange load.

In the Třebíč school, the assembly point for the transports, we were given camp numbers. That was the last time that we were together with our Mohelno grandmother and gentle Aunt Greta, Mother's younger sister. We were separated in the train, and they were transported from Terezín "to the east" and their death in 1942. My brother and I remained in Terezín till the autumn of 1944. Then we too were put into transports going to Auschwitz. But by a miracle we both survived the seven months to the end of the war.

In Terezín I was first put into the Sudeten barracks. In the spring of 1942 we were not yet allowed to leave the buildings. Surrounded by strange faces, I knew nothing of the fate of my parents, relatives, or friends. The days passed in anxious waiting. On July 6, 1942, movement in the streets of the ghetto was permitted. The prisoners were allowed to leave the barracks and the streets of Terezín filled with crowds, each person searching the faces for someone they knew. I moved through this throng not knowing where to go and what to do.

Those several scores of boys, all about thirteen years old, who later met in Home Number One of L 417, were a very specific group, different from the other homes in the former Terezín school. The decisive factor was age. With the exception of Home Five, we were the only ones in L 417 who had reached a critical age in our development. When the German occupation began in 1938, we were already too mature to escape into a child's micro-world, to have our consciousness clouded by a childish fear of ill-treatment. Everything that happened to us made us grow up faster, at least psychologically. We had witnessed the destruction of our homes, the helplessness of our parents. Marked by stars and numbers, in quarantine and in the Schleusen,* we saw conventions destroyed, and witnessed the ardor and fragility and finiteness of human relationships, we saw altruism and naked selfishness, we listened to the death rattle of the dying and the heavy breathing of couples having sex.

And this was how Valtr Eisinger found us. He was still very young himself, only twenty-nine. He was not a brilliant man, just a talented teacher at the beginning of his career. He hadn't yet been given the chance to stretch his abilities, to clarify his views of life and the world. He was still busy with himself, and now wanted above all to help us. And so he took counsel from his literature, his poets, his older and more experienced friend, Dr. Bruno Zwicker. We loved his enthusiastic courage, his certainty in this fragile world of the camp, and announced: "After the war I shall try for my Doctorate." We felt close to him because we wanted to be like him, this wonderful teacher who talked to us about the philosophy of Mahatma Gandhi, translated poems, played football, moved into a bunk in our home, sang in *The Bartered Bride*, and loved his Terezín wife, Věra, with all his heart. We could laugh at his faults, but they only brought him closer to us. The knowledge of our common fate, and Eisinger's personality, enabled us to establish a community that included orphanage boys as well as the son of a scientist or a self-assured son of a luxury car dealer. This spirit pervades every page of our magazine.

VEDEM, Terezín 1942–1944

It Happened
One Evening

I have an acquaintance, may God grant him eternal glory, quite a good fellow, but with one great advantage. He once confided in me, in complete confidence, that he had … an uncle in the Gestapo. Well, not every Jew has such a *mishpoche** so I must keep on the good side of him.

After a time we got talking about this uncle of his again.

– So how about your uncle?

– I got it wrong, he was in the SS.

– There's quite a difference, isn't there?

– Well, the Gestapo's like the SS in plain clothes.

– I wouldn't say that.

– No, but a lot of people think so.

– What did he do there?

– He was in charge of their cars.

– What?

– You know, he was in charge of the cars of the people who keep things in order. But he got paid by the SS and had a pass for the tram.

– Oh I see, he was a Jew?

– What did you think he was?

– A German.

– Go wash your mouth out.

Suddenly a voice can be heard, coming from one of the bunks:

– Can you get me a grandmother in the Gestapo?

– It's better than having a horse.

A voice of the people:

– I hear the oat rations have been cut. What are you going to eat?

– Sheeeet.

The SS man's nephew:

– Horse, schmorse.

– Get me a granny in the Gestapo.

– It's got to be better than having a horse.

– Not necessarily. What would you rather have, horses or a granny in the Gestapo?

– You're the horse.

– I can't be a horse, can I?

– That was good, we'll put it in the paper!

– Jiří Bruml

Jan Klein
(b. 1930, perished).
"The Railway Station."
Crayons, 300 × 205 mm.
Jewish Museum, Prague,
Inv. No. 121653.

Rambles
Through Terezín

When we hear the word Kinderküche, what immediately springs to mind is the serving hatch in the yard of L 318. The children's kitchen seems to us like a dark hole leading into a strange land where cooks, both male and female, rush about in white smocks and whence wisps of steam emerge.

It seemed quite different to Šnajer and me when we had a thorough look at it, talked to the master cook Rabl, and had him explain everything to us. We had to wait a while for him. All that time, figures passed by hefting hundred kilo sacks of flour and other foodstuffs, strapping wenches carrying trays of buns, the robust figure of Mr. Bachner, the muscular servers of black coffee, and in the midst of all that Mr. Karvan, the commander-in-chief of the children's bakery, walking nonchalantly up and down in a grey raincoat with his hair combed back. Every now and then master cook Rabl flashed past like lightning.

Finally, after running about for some time, he stopped, looked round to see if there was anything else to do, and then said at last, "All right, boys, I've finally got time for you." And this is how our interview began:

"How big is the staff in the children's

* From the Hebrew and
Yiddish: family, relatives.

kitchen?"

"Fifty-four persons including the bakery and all the porters."

"What equipment do you have?"

"Five boilers; three for smoke and two for steam (for a pressure of .4 atmospheres). Apart from that we have a confectioner's oven. We have eighteen mixing troughs and twelve barrels."

"How many people do you cook for?"

"Three thousand children from the barracks and the blocks."

"How big are the batches?"

"For instance, we prepare three hundred liters of coffee in the morning, two hundred and fifty kilograms of millet, one thousand eight hundred liters of soup at lunchtime and one thousand five hundred in the evening."

"How long before serving do you have to start cooking? And do you have night shifts?"

"That depends on the menu. Sometimes we have to start two days in advance, sometimes a day ahead, and naturally we work through the night. Not long ago we were working right up to six o'clock in the morning, cutting up six hundred and thirty kilos of spinach."

"That was the time we had it with dumplings, wasn't it? We got large portions of spinach then, didn't we?"

"And you probably didn't even realize what a job we had to separate and wash that spinach."

We were silent with embarrassment. Indeed, the cooks' work is sometimes difficult and unpleasant. But on the other hand, the atmosphere in the kitchen is excellent, jokes are bandied about, and sometimes they even break out in song. In this respect Mr. Karvan is in a class by himself.

Having had all our questions answered, we thanked Mr. Rabl and went home.

– Academy (*Unknown author*)

Rambles
Through Terezín

At the same time as we visited the Kinder-küche, Šnajer and I also looked in on the children's bakery. There we found Mr. Karvan, who was kind enough to show us everything.

"How much stuff do you need for the buns?"

"That varies; for the last batch, for instance, we used two hundred and fifty kilograms of fine-ground flour."

"How much margarine and sugar do you put into your dough? How long before serving do you start baking? How large is your staff?" Our questions came hard and fast.

Mr. Karvan smiled at our interest and said, "As to your first question, about ten percent of the bun dough is margarine and sugar. We have to start baking the day before. We have a staff of ten in the bakery."

"And how large is your oven?"

"60 by 40. We have three such ovens that hold about four hundred and eighty buns at once."

"How much coal do you need? Do you get anthracite or brown coal?"

"Brown coal, of course. We use two hundredweight a day, sometimes more."

"I have often wondered why there are sometimes bits of margarine floating about in the sauce we get with our dumplings. Is that due to bad mixing?"

"Certainly not. Sometimes we add more margarine to the sauce to make it thinner, and then it doesn't get absorbed because there is too much of it. It can't be properly mixed with the other ingredients."

"And what are these other ingredients?"

"Flour, sugar, cocoa, and milk. Then the mixture is steamed. And then the margarine is added."

We had no more questions and so we had a look round the bakery. The heat from the oven hit us and every now and then a half-naked baker would take out a baking sheet full of golden buns and put them on a nearby shelf to cool. In the meantime I drew a sketch of the oven (using Šnajer as a desk). "We also have pretty girls here," said Mr. Karvan, patting one of the cooks on the back. "The only problem is they make bubbles in the pastry. But don't mention that in your magazine."

Wouldn't dream of it, I promised. We said goodbye and, nearly tripping over a trough full of potatoes standing in the way, left the children's kitchen.

– Academy (*Unknown author*)

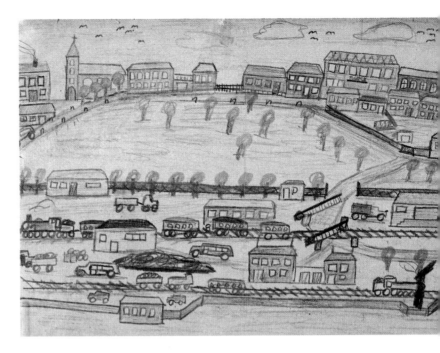

Josef Kraus
(b. 1931, perished).
"The Town."
Crayons, 300 × 215 mm.
Jewish Museum, Prague,
Inv. No. 1221521.

Zentralbad*

Having obtained a red or white ticket with the letter M or J, I take my towel, soap, and washcloth and go to Vrchlabí – the main bathhouse. There I join a group of men or boys waiting for the gates to open. If the group consists of men I listen to the latest guaranteed accurate news, and if they are boys, I get up-to-date reports on the Terezín sports scene, or on girls, or suchlike. Suddenly the gates open, the group starts to move and I with them. A man appears who wants to see my ticket, checks it and then lets me in with the words: "Get your clogs and get moving!" I take a few steps, then a boy stops me and directs me to a room. When I enter, I see a number of benches and pegs. I take off my clothes because there are only people of my sex here and there's no reason to be bashful. Then I go to a man who examines my hair and body before letting me go under the shower. Later I heard him referred to as the delouser, or something like that. When I tried to find out more about him I was told that he was an elderly physician who no longer practiced and who worked in the *Gesundheitswesen*** department. If I'm one of the last there's no free shower any more – I'm at the mercy of my companions. The Zentralbad has two shower rooms and one pool where people are rarely allowed in. In each room a boy turns on the water: this is done twice at seven-minute intervals. In between you have to soap yourself down. When

* Main bath.
** Department of self-administration for health care in the camp.

104

the bath is over cold water is let in, but only a few brave souls can stand under it. Some of the boys always go for their bath in the evening because sometimes, if they're lucky, they can get into the pool even without a ticket. Since I don't know what else to write, I am finishing my commentary.

– Medic Šnajer (*Jiří Grünbaum*)

Rambles Through Terezín

Today we bring you a report from the doctor in charge of the home for babies and toddlers in Terezín. Before beginning the report proper, we would like to give you some data to think about. 25,000 persons have died in the ghetto, 92 children were born, present inhabitants number 43,000, and so far 100,000 persons have passed through the ghetto.

Babies in Terezín!

Like most of the other children in Terezín, our smallest, the infants and toddlers, are placed in a single home especially suitable for them. That is in the houses near the "Prague" road, with a view of parkland. About one hundred and eighty children between the ages of two weeks and eighteen months live here, as close as possible to their mothers, who stay in rooms specially assigned to them. Some of these babies came to us on the transports, some were born in Terezín and were sent to us from the maternity ward from ten to fourteen days after their birth.

The nurseries are very pretty, usually full of sunshine, and the children have every comfort that can be afforded them in Terezín. Each one of them has a pretty little cot, a shelf, there is a table in the room, a wash basin, a sink for dishes, a small side table with a medicine chest, chairs, scales. The mothers and the nurses see to it that the children are clean and the rooms tidy.

In the homes there is also what is called a milk kitchen, where the food for the babies is prepared. Then there is a collection point for the laundry, which is sent almost daily to the central laundry, and returned. There is a branch station of Youth Care with a nice supply of clothing and underwear, diapers, a sewing room for mending the children's laundry, and of course the inevitable administrative office. This office, for the time being, houses the pharmacy. Small children need constant care and this is why their mothers are exempt from labor. Furthermore about sixty trained nurses are employed, taking twelve-hour shifts. Several physicians monitor the children's health, most of them specialists, some of whom live in the home. We also have a nice clinic which, however, is hardly ever used by the babies. They are usually seen by the doctors in the rooms where they live.

How do such tiny creatures live and how do they spend their day? They usually wake up early, then they have their morning bath, get their breakfast, that is, they are breast fed by their mothers, or they get some broth, then they are put back to bed, where they can amuse themselves as they like, depending on their temperament. The bawlers bawl, some sleep, some coo, some observe their surroundings and behave like little monkeys in a cage. A healthy child is a lovely creature and a joy to look at and observe. At ten o'clock they get their next feeding, then comes the major doctor's round, then there are the daily walks. The day passes in the wink of an eye. Normally the babies are fed five times a day, the last time being at ten o'clock in the evening. Naturally there are exceptions to the rule every day, for the children may be ill, and we have even had epidemics of children's diseases that claimed a substantial number of lives.

What a joy it is to look at a healthy child, and what a sad sight a sick baby is. The child is helpless and cannot say where it hurts. It's entirely up to the nursing staff to recognize what is wrong with the little patient, to diagnose the problem and to act in time. From what has been written it may be seen that in Terezín everything possible, under the circumstances, is being done for the babies. The children are mostly doing well, and if you happen to glance into a pram passing in the street, you will see a healthy, tanned, pretty child.

Still, we can only hope their situation will soon change, and that they will be given a chance to grow up in a healthier environment, like other children.

– Dr. G. A. (*Unknown author*)

In 1942 the "Council of Elders" decided that the children should receive larger and more nourishing portions of food. The prisoners looking after them tried every way they could to keep them alive for a future life in freedom.

A little over two hundred children were born in Terezín. Many died shortly after birth. Most were not allowed to be born at all. From August 1943 on the SS men ruthlessly ordered abortions and if a birth was kept secret, families were sent off with the next transport. The liquidation transports in the autumn of 1944 took away an overwhelming number of the children who had until then survived in Terezín.

"The birth was easy... Now everything is all right. All right? My wife gave birth to her baby in a room in the barracks, on a borrowed iron bed, and three hours later she had to return to her lodgings..." This is how a former Terezín prisoner, a physician from Brno, remembers his experience in Terezín. The child was born in April 1942. On October 19, 1944, mother and child were deported to Auschwitz where they were gassed.

Only twenty-five of the children born in Terezín lived to see liberation...

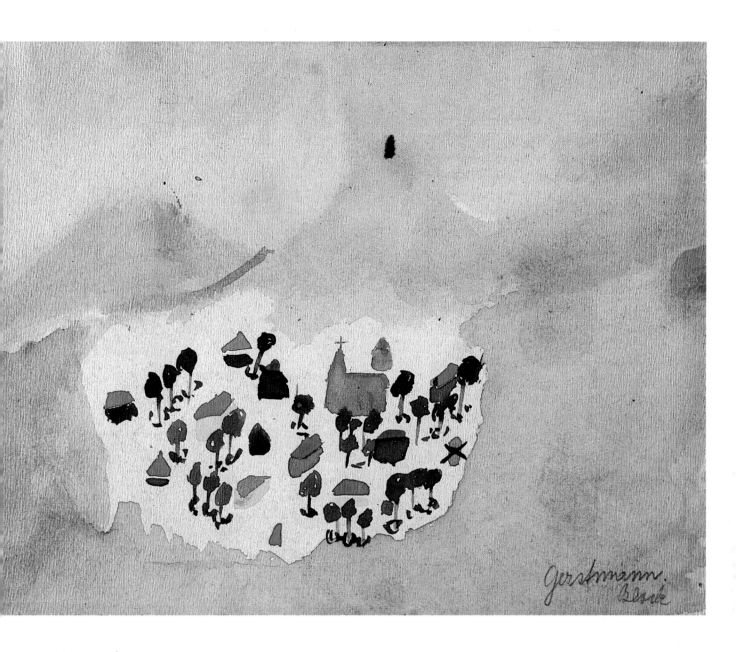

Margit Gerstmanová
(b. 1931, perished).
"Landscape."
Aquarelle, 275 × 210 mm.
Jewish Museum, Prague,
Inv. No. 133422.

VEDEM, Terezín 1943

With You, Mother

In filth and sludge and hunger, we suffer here,
Cast into a pit of darkness, of infinite pain,
Held down by our masters, deprived of our rights,
Mother mine, we shall walk forever together.

We shall walk toward the sun, though tired and weary
We shall walk with courage in our brethren's footsteps,
Walk on, though our bodies be numb from the beating,
We shall walk to the east through the pools of blood.

We shall walk to a distant place, far beyond mountains,
Into a clean world, a world of equality,
Into a world where freedom's flags fly,
And all former ills are long forgotten.

We shall come to our goal, no matter how distant
Fresh smiles on our faces, the race we shall win.
Dear Mother, we'll be with you forever and ever,
In freedom to live, and our rights to enjoy.

– Orče (*Zdeněk Ornest*)

The first transport – Ak – arrived in Terezín on November 24, 1941. The job was to prepare the town for the tens of thousands of inhabitants who would soon be arriving. This transport was followed immediately by several more, however, and there was nowhere to lodge the people. At that time Terezín still had its own civilian population. The prisoners were put into barracks, which they were not allowed to leave without permission. They were even forbidden to have any contact whatsoever with their families. Once a week, a detail of local constables took the children to visit their parents. The civilian population was removed from Terezín at the beginning of July 1942, and the entire town was turned into a concentration camp.

VEDEM, Terezín 1942
Friday Evening

How long since I saw Hradčany, bathed in the sun?
How long since I was a human being?
But I wonder today, was it all just a dream?

A year now I've been in the Terezín ghetto,
A year now I've watched a people destroyed,
A year now I've stared at walls cracking and peeling.

Before, when the constable guarded the barracks,
And no one could enter, and no one could leave,
His bayonet was fixed, and his eyes full of anger
He stared at the streets of Terezín.

Saturday…
The barracks seething with people,
The yard full of children.
What's going on?

The children will go
To their waiting mothers
When the "forward march" is given.

The constable walks by them
With rifle and bayonet.
At last they stand by the women's barracks
But the command is now given – "Go back."

Sadly the children leave their mothers,
Mothers they did not even see.
It's always this way, with everything.
Daily portions of turnips and coffee,
Daily, dozens of people die.
Why?
Why? Why do the innocent die?

But the day will come when all this will end,
The day will come when we shall live again,
The day will come when we shall settle accounts.

– Written, while he had typhoid, by Kangaroo (*Zdeněk Weinberger*)

Thoughts

I stood at the corner and looked in the window
To a place where heart is divided from heart
On the bed lay Had's limp shadows,
When a madman suddenly lifted his hand, crying:
"Mummy!…
Mummy, come here, let's play together
And kiss and talk to each other!"
Poor people, madmen, miserable figures,
Wrapped against the weather, they went
Shivering with cold, and wanting to shout
Before their days were done:

"Mummy, hold me, I'm a leaf about to fall.
Look how I wither, I feel so cold!"
As the awful chorale echoed across the barracks,
I – swept up in it – sing along with them.

– Ha- (*Hanuš Hachenburg*)

Families were separated on arrival in Terezín. The men lived in the men's barracks, the women in theirs. Later on, so-called "children's homes" were also established.

VEDEM, Terezín 1943
Farewell to Summer

I should like to write as you do, poets,
Of spring's end, of love and sunny days,
Of tender evenings spent in the moonlight
Of birds and flowers, of trees in bud.

I should like to say farewell, as you who are free,
With a walk in the woods, with a river, and fruit,
As in times of old when we were like you are
When I was not, as today, broken and forlorn.

I would like to take leave of the summer as you do,
In the sun, stopped short by my prison grate,
To fondle a fading bud for a while –
I cannot, I cannot – for I live behind bars.

– Orče (*Zdeněk Ornest*)

The acknowledged poets of Shkid were Hanuš Hachenburg (1929–1944), who mostly signed himself Ha-, and Zdeněk Ohrenstein (Ornest), nicknamed Orče and Mustafa.

Zdeněk Ohrenstein was born on January 10, 1929, in Kutná Hora, the third son of Berta and Eduard Ohrenstein. This family has a permanent place in the history of Czech literature because they gave to it Jiří Orten, after whose tragic death in 1941 František Halas wrote:

> "When fish swim in cathedrals
> this poet
> will be remembered by name."

The environment in which Ota, Jiří and Zdeněk Ohrenstein grew up was described by Ota Ornest in his commemorative article "My Brother," included in *The Diaries of Jiří Orten*, published by the Czechoslovak Writers' Publishing House in 1958.

"Our father Eduard was an unusually serious, quiet, and oversensitive person, especially considering the business atmosphere in which he grew up and lived. He was born in 1881 in Zruč nad Sázavou and, as was usual in those days, came from a large family. Because of his outstanding abilities, he was the only one who was sent to the grammar school in Kutná Hora. He boarded with relatives in Nové Dvory and every Sunday he walked home to Zruč and back again. But the relatives in Nové Dvory had many children of their own and Eduard spent more time looking after them than he did at school. In any case the money for further studies ran out in three years, so Eduard became an apprentice in Dvůr Králové nad Labem, where he remained for eighteen years. In the early years of our century he was one of the seven founding members of a social democratic party in Dvůr Králové, a party to which he was to remain faithful for the rest of his life. In 1921, after a very short acquaintance, he married Berta. It was an arranged marriage, as the custom was then. The couple settled in Kutná Hora, where Eduard bought a business from Berta's uncle using money he had saved up in Dvůr Králové; it took him years to repay his debt.

"Berta was born in 1890 in Neustupov near Tábor. Her family was larger than Eduard's, though somewhat better situated. Her brother, Josef Rosenzweig-Moir, completed his law studies in Prague and became a friend of Hašek, Mahen, and Brunner. He published two collections of poems (*The Garden of Life*; *When Youth Sings*).

"For two years Berta also went to school in Prague. Her great talent for the theater became evident there, but a girl like her could only marry into a decent family; anything else was unheard of. She married a man she hardly knew and it was the most wonderful marriage in the world. Father loved Mother with a love never expressed in words, but was evident in every other way, and Mother was worthy of his love. They were often in grave financial straits – the little house with the shop in Kollár Street almost had to be auctioned off – but the children were hardly aware of it, for they came above everything else. Father raised us with kind words and without physical punishment. He wrote long, encouraging letters, even when he was already seriously ill and Jiří was in Prague. "It is strange," Jiří wrote in a letter after Father's death, "I cannot recollect that Father ever uttered a lie, not even in the most negligible matter."

"Mother was full of life and vigor… * Thanks to her, laughter was the driving force in our lives. She had a vivid imagination and the children hung on her every word when she would invent stories for them. Daily life with her was never monotonous. She never nursed a sense of

* She died in 1970.

112

grievance or self-pity, not even when the Nazis came and Father was no longer alive.

"Mother filled Jiří's childhood with yet another love that enveloped all the members of our family – her love for the theater. She was an enthusiastic amateur actor, the soul of the Kutná Hora little theater. She lived for the theater. Each new role became a fascinating adventure for the whole family, even when the boys were still too young to go to the theater and could only witness her practicing her part at home in the evening. They were chased out of the rehearsals they sometimes tried to sneak into, and on the evening of the premiere they huddled together in bed and told each other how beautiful and successful Mother was. And Father wrote about the theater for the Social Democratic paper Podvysocko, where he worked in the editorial office.

"In Father we lost a man of the most upright character. Everything he did was filled with a sense of great moral responsibility. How were we to make up for this loss? Only in the belief that the gaping hole he left behind did not exist, that his moral example would live forever."

Marie: You were seven when your father died. Did anything change in your life after that?
Zdeněk: Father's death was a great shock for the whole family. Both my brothers had moved away from Kutná Hora at the time and I was left alone with Mother. I would say that Father's death put an end to my childhood, which had been very happy indeed.
Marie: What happened then?
Zdeněk: I went on living in Kutná Hora until I was ten, then the Germans came, took everything we had, banned a lot of things. I was not allowed to study at the grammar school for which I had passed the entrance exam. For one year I lived a life full of incomprehensible ups and downs, my friends were forced to shun me, I was not allowed to go anywhere. I remember I literally wanted to die once when I could not resist and snuck into the movies. A few hooligans began shouting, "Jews out, Jews out!" and I had to flee in shame. Then, because things kept getting worse, Mother managed to get me into the Jewish Orphanage in Prague.
Marie: When was that?
Zdeněk: About Christmas 1940. That meant I could go to the Jewish Secondary School and be among friends and teachers who were afflicted in the same way. Under those conditions, a child could live more freely, relatively speaking. I was terribly homesick for Mother, because actually we were no longer allowed to meet. I saw her only once, when she came to Jiří's funeral, and she had to have a special permit from the Gestapo. I did get used to it after some time, I made friends with the boys there, I found a wonderful buddy in Hanuš Hachenburg, who was also my close friend in Terezín when we were deported along with the other boys from the orphanage in October 1942. So after two years, I met my Mother again. She'd been in the camp since June 1942. I don't really have to say anything about our life in Terezín. It's all in our magazine.
Marie: But you didn't stay in Terezín till the end of the war?
Zdeněk: No, I was sent out on the second last of the final transports, the ninth out of ten, and got to Auschwitz on October 19, 1944, bearing the number Es 1017.
Marie: So you were fifteen. How did you manage to escape being selected for the gas chambers? I thought everyone under eighteen was gassed?
Zdeněk: By sheer chance, which can be said in general about my survival, and in fact about the survival of the adult prisoners as well. In my

case it was just damned good luck. Doctor Mengele, who made the selection on the platform of the Auschwitz station, had actually put me on the side destined for the gas chambers, along with the old people, mothers with children, the sick, and children who were alone. Nobody had the slightest idea what this selection meant. But some of my older friends were in the group lined up a few dozen meters away, and they waved me over. I managed to join them without the least idea what I had escaped from. It was only in Camp E that I learned what it was all about.

Marie: And after that?

Zdeněk: You know, so much has been written about the terror of the concentration camps that everybody has a pretty good idea of what it was like. My case was special in that I found myself in an environment of the most terrible cruelty at an immature age, oversensitive, going through puberty, alone, far more helpless than the adults around me. I had to come face to face with death and suffering in all its inhuman forms, watch people die who were far fitter and stronger than I was, look on when they beat my fellow prisoners to death, hanged them and tortured them, live through all the epidemics, including paratyphoid, lie for several hours in a railway wagon covered by corpses and, during the most terrible times of hunger, conceal the death of the comrade lying next to me as long as possible so that I could get his rations, too, at least for a few days. And I lived through all this at an age when we normally fall in love for the first time, learn to dance, read lyric poetry, and play football. Recollections of life in Terezín became a beautiful dream that ended, as paradoxical as that may seem.

Marie: Did you meet anyone from Number One there?

Zdeněk: In Auschwitz I caught sight of Professor Eisinger marching by in a column and he was in such a terrible state that it took my breath away. It was a terrible feeling not to be able to find anyone in this inferno to turn to for support. Otherwise I saw nobody from Shkid. I was usually together in the blocks with Poles, Greeks, and Hungarians.

Marie: When were you liberated?

Zdeněk: In the early days of May, 1945, a few days before Prague was liberated. It was in Dachau, where they'd taken us from Kaufering because the Allied armies were approaching. We learned later that we were to have been taken thirty kilometers behind the front and shot in accordance with Himmler's orders "not to let one living prisoner fall into enemy hands." But in Dachau, after a three-day journey in open trucks in winter and in rain, they had to release us on the order of the International Red Cross, which had its representatives there at the time. Then everything was simple. After a month of quarantine and delousing they sent us home.

Marie: What were your feelings like?

Zdeněk: Indescribable. It took me some time before I learned to walk through parks, ride in the front carriages of the Prague streetcars, use cutlery, not hoard food continuously, and in general, to behave in a civilized manner. I had to learn slowly to live like the people around me and not to feel like a terrified little animal.

After the war sixteen-year-old Zdeněk met his mother again. She had remained in Terezín saved from the transports because she'd been sent to work in the "Glimmer" factory, peeling mica. Then he was also reunited with his brother Ota, who returned from Great Britain where he had worked in the Czechoslovak resistance abroad. Only Jirka – the poet Jiří Orten – was missing.

Hardly anybody else in this large family survived the fascist fury. In October, 1944, their uncle – the poet Josef Rosenzweig-Moir – had also died in the gas chambers of Auschwitz.

At the Crossroads

Where can I rest my soul, where let my body carry me?
What should I toil for, where should I sow my seed?
I lean over you, I stand at the crossroads,
The wall crumbles under me, my load weighs me down.

A thousand unknown voices call me from afar,
Whatever I aim at I cannot attain,
A terrible loneliness chokes me to death,
And everyone waits for the funeral pyre.

What use are the calluses, the weatherworn faces,
Proudly waiting for old age to come?
What use is this fading, this piteous sobbing,
Idleness, indifference, what are they to us?

Where can we turn, and to whom surrender?
Where seek salvation, in whom to believe?
Whose advice can we take, and who will return?
Oh, who will pity us, treat us with trust?

Who gave us life to live to the full?
Why must we die when we just want to live?
Before going forward our footsteps would falter.
Our bell is now tolling, and we don't want to die!

I woefully ask myself, where shall I turn to?
Where is my place now, and where will I stand?
I have not gone far. Now I stand at the crossroads
And do not know what I'm to make of my life.

– Orče (*Zdeněk Ornest*)

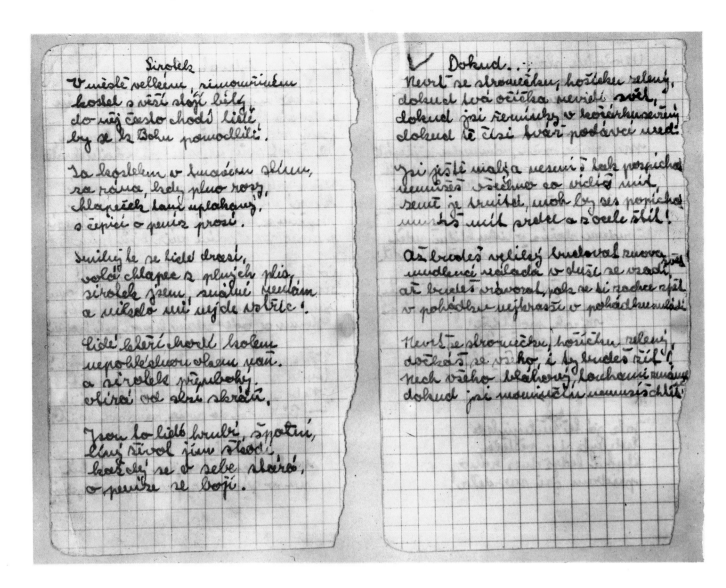

Manuscript of the Terezín poems "The Orphan" and "As long as …" by **Zdeněk Ohrenstein (Ornest)**. Jewish Museum, Prague, Neg. No. 27714.

The Forgotten

(Dedicated to Ruth N., a girl who immediately on our arrival at Terezín was sent on to Poland.)

You pale remembrance compels me to be calm,
That once again I may recall my love,
Perhaps I'll smile again when we embrace
You are my ally, and my best of friends.

Sweet remembrance, tell me a fairy tale
Of my beloved that now is lost to me.
Tell me the story of the Golden Glitter,
And tell the swallow to come back to me.

Fly after her and whisper it in her ear.
Does she remember me, even for a moment?
Is she well, and even more I'd know –
Am I still her one and only love?

Come quickly back to me, don't lose your way,
I would recall other memories from the past.
Beautiful you were, but I fear that you're gone.
Goodbye my love. I loved you once so well.

– Orče (*Zdeněk Ornest*)

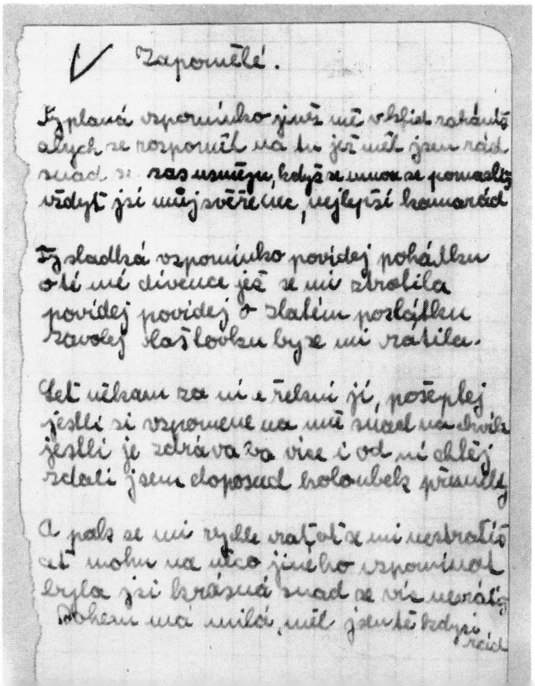

Manuscript of the Terezín poem "The Forgotten" by **Zdeněk Ohrenstein (Ornest)**. Jewish Museum, Prague, Neg. No. 27688/b.

117

Petr Ginz
(b. 1928, perished)
"Kavalír Barracks":
illustration to a chapter
of his serial "Rambles
Through Terezín."
Pencil, 128 × 44 mm.
Memorial of Terezín,
Vedem p. 76.

Rambles
Through Terezín

Once my guide and I visited the Kavalír barracks.* I entered ostentatiously on the left. The steward in the gate couldn't have cared less whether I walked on the left or on the right. I don't suppose he'd have minded if I'd walked on my head. Then I went smartly up to Dr. Kelly, the commandant of the Kavalír *Ordnerwache*.

– Good day, Dr. Kelly, I'm the editor of the magazine *Vedem*. I've taken the liberty of coming to see you to ask you a few questions.

(Dr. Kelly welcomed me affably. Unlike many such officials, he is a pleasant man who tries not to behave officiously, but to be kind and friendly to everyone, even to a busybody editor like me.)

– Could you please tell me what the task of the *Ordnerwache* is, and how it differs from that of the *Ghettowache*?

– There's no great difference. Both are responsible for keeping order in the ghetto. But the *Ghettowache* sees more to security and carrying out of orders from above. It also acts as criminal police force. The *Ordnerwache*, on the other hand, looks after cleanliness, discipline, and related matters. The men on duty in the yard go after the people who spit, litter, spill water, or have their eiderdowns hanging out of the window after eight a.m. They supervise the toilets and the pump. The guard on duty at the gate gives information, sees to it that people walk on the right (we laugh) and checks passes. And he sees to security and order at the gate.

– How many stewards do barracks like Magdeburg, for instance, need?

– About sixty.

– Thank you, Dr. Kelly, for your information.

– My pleasure. I'm glad to hear that the young people in the children's homes are involved in cultural activities like your magazine.

Then Dr. Kelly started to ask questions about our magazine and about our life in general. I answered his questions in detail. I said goodbye to the affable commandant of the *Ordnerwache*, found my way through several rooms and came out into the fresh air. I noticed that not one door knob was working properly. That is one thing no *Ordnerwache*, or *Ghettowache* nor any other *Wache* is looking after.

– nz (*Petr Ginz*)

* A building that is part of the old fortifications.

Rambles
Through Terezín

One day, when I was reminded it was time to write another of my Rambles through Terezín, I thought I might do something about our security forces.* I put this plan into practice on Friday after inspection, when Lebenhart and I set out for the Dresden constabulary. We were welcomed in a friendly manner by chief officer A. His first question was whether our paper was anything like the *České slovo*, because he was a National Socialist.

He invited us to sit down on the bench and ask questions. He could speak about the *Ghettowache* all night long, he said. Then he started to tell us that the *Ghettowache* consisted of two hundred men, that their commander was Captain Meisl and his second-in-command Tackenheim. Under them are four Section commanders (*Abteilungsleiter*) and two patrol officers, and they in turn have platoon leaders under them (commanders of the guard), and they have two seconds-in-command, with the rank of chief officer (deputy commanders of the guard). Then he explained that the duties of the ghetto policeman were allocated according to a duty roster that is always available at the police station for the commander in case of inspection, so that he knows where his officers are at any given time.

From under a heap of papers and notebooks, he pulled a board to which a piece of paper inscribed with various squares and figures was affixed. While he was explaining what it all meant, the door opened and a plump woman walked in. She turned out

to be the chief officer's daughter, and she was bringing her father his supper. Undisturbed, he continued. Then his daughter interrupted him, saying that he was not quite right. Naturally that annoyed him and he asked her not to interfere, then went on with his explanation, while constantly pointing out that "all this was strictly off the record."

When he had finished explaining the roster sheet he talked about the duties and rights of the *Ghettowache*. It was like a police force in that it had powers of arrest. The commanding officer, Captain W., even had the right to punish slander and lesser offenses by disciplinary sentences of imprisonment up to a week, or a fine. Cases involving longer sentences had to be passed on to the KRIPO,** or Criminal Police. Serious cases are passed on to the *Ghettogericht*,*** which operates according to the legal system of the Protectorate. With some pride he told us that the ghetto policeman on duty at the ghetto borders collaborates with the constable, and that they check up on each other.

Then he described the procedure for reporting the escape of a ghetto inmate. At half past ten at night everybody must be at home. If not, it is the duty of the room elder to report the absence to the house elder, whose duty in turn it is to report it to the nearest guardroom. From there a report is immediately sent to the KRIPO, and then it is passed on to the Council of Elders. They report it to the *Dienststelle* (duty office), who in turn inform the constabulary, who immediately surround the ghetto and the neighboring districts. There is a garrison of two hundred constables in the ghetto for this purpose. He went on to tell us that the *Ghettowache* also delivers summonses papers and directs the transports, which is their most embarrass-

* The article describes the security and legal system established by the prison self-administration.
** Kriminalpolizei – plainclothes police.
*** Ghetto law court.

ing task. He further told us that the *Ghettowache* was divided into two rotas (formerly five companies) of a hundred men each. These are further subdivided into watches, one each for Magdeburg (first district), Hamburg (second district), and the German House (third district),* where the main watch, and therefore the largest number of men, is stationed, and Dresden (fourth district). The Magdeburg and Dresden watches are also in charge of the ghetto prisons.

At this point he pulled a gray notebook out from under a heap. It had the letter M (male) on one side of the cover, and F (female) on the other side. This was to show us how the number of prisoners is kept track of, and what is written about the individual prisoners. We were interrupted by one of the officials from the KRIPO, who requested four men to go on guard duty in the prisoners' washroom. Having issued the necessary orders, the duty officer again sat down with us and started to explain how the *Ghettowache* collaborated with the other sections of the *Sicherheitswesen*.** He told us "quite in confidence" that five short blows on the whistle meant that the ghetto policeman was calling for help.

Promotions are granted not only according to service but also according to progress in school where laws and new regulations are taught. In summer they also hold maneuvers. Then he boasted that the *Ghettowache* was also the proud owner of a pontoon bridge that could be used in case of flooding.

When I had learned enough I said goodbye and the ghetto policemen said they would like to see a copy of our paper. With this we took leave of the guardians of our safety.

– H. M. (*probably Herbert Maier*)

Ghetto Cops

Since Terezín is trying hard to imitate the outside world in everything, it was essential to have some guardians of the peace. This is why the *Ordnerwache*, popularly called the ghetto cops, was established. A ghetto cop is of the male sex, wears a heavy winter coat with a wide belt to which a stick called a truncheon is attached. He wears dark breeches and heavy boots. He has a band fixed to his shoulder with the letter W and a number. He has the same symbol inscribed on a metal badge that swings on his chest. The most characteristic part of the ghetto cop's uniform is his high cap with a badge and stripes indicating his rank.

But enough of the description. Let us proceed to the daily work of such a ghetto cop. Some stand at the crossroads and don't let anybody pass who does not give them a cigarette. It is a most advantageous business and a ghetto "traffic" cop always has a guaranteed supply of cigarettes.

Another type of these guardians of disorder stands in the gates to the barracks shouting "Rechts gehen!" (walk on the right) all day and all night. But since the cop on barrack duty is at a disadvantage compared with his colleague from the crossroads, he earns his daily bread in the following way: At least twice a day he introduces *Kasernensperre****** and lets only physicians and nursing staff through. Don't get me wrong, this is not because they are the guardians of our health, it's just because they are people who have tobacco.

The third type of ghetto cop lounges about on the streets, and wherever anything happens they rush in, start to shout, swear and get more in the way than anyone else.

A favorite amusement of the ghetto cops is to walk through the streets (they call it marching) or to parade before Löwenstein****** and bring shame on their calling.

Long live the new Reservists.

(*Unknown author*)

* Today the House of Culture on the town square of Terezín.
** Security Department.
*** Entry to barracks forbidden.
**** Commandant of the prison ghetto guards.

Unknown artist
"Ghettowache."
Aquarelle, 145 × 210 mm.
Jewish Museum, Prague,
Inv. No. 129186.

The Cap
(A Feuilleton)

A small, insignificant cap, but nevertheless in Terezín it is of the greatest importance. It is enough to go out into the street and watch the caps passing by to learn something about their owners. A high cap with a badge and one or two yellow stripes clearly indicates that its owner is a ghetto cop, one of the enforcers of order in Terezín. We recognize firemen, who have not yet put out a fire and are hardly ever likely to do so, by their forage caps. If you meet a man in a white cap try to get into his good books, because believe me, that man, usually corpulent, is a cook. If you make his acquaintance, you are not likely to die of starvation. But you must not mistake the *Leichenträger** for a cook, for they wear similar clothes. Last but not least, if you see a beret with a little stem on top, you know at once that its owner is an inhabitant of the *Jugendkaserne*** I. The poor chap is hiding his closely shaven head, the result of a barber's rough and ready ministrations. A fashionable lady's hat covers the tricolor hair of a young miss, lady or old woman: the hair is blonde in front, black in the middle and the back, and gray hair shines through.

People arriving or leaving with a transport have up to twenty-five different types of warm caps on their heads. German Jews prefer a special type of cap with a peak, which the Czechs (except for Baron Münchhausen) do not wear.

What I have written here is only a tiny fragment of what could be said of the caps in Terezín. Since there is no more space I must finish.

– Abscess (*Jiří Bruml*)

* Corpse bearers.
** Barracks where young
people were lodged.

Parademarsch
Ghettowache
in the Dresden Barracks

Tah rah rah boom dee ay!

The crowds are tightly packed in the Dresden Barracks. Aging gray-haired old women grin from the windows, as well as sniggering boys and smirking young ladies. You can see the shining faces of important personalities and the unshaven faces of old men. A few brave ones are even sitting on the roof.

Tah rah rah boom dee yay!

"Ghettowache, stillgestanden" (Ghetto watch, halt). The band is playing. The conductor stands in front waving his baton. *"Abteilung marsch"* (Section, march), shouts the man with two stripes on his cap. The stamping of feet can be heard in the front entrance. Look, here's a man with piping down his trouser legs and epaulettes on his shoulders, behind him two commandants, then a captain and two sergeants. They are leading a group of about twenty dedicated ghetto cops in light blue uniforms. (In Haiti, there are 5,000 generals and 2,000 soldiers.) The company sways to the rhythm of the band and finally get themselves in line in the right place. At that moment the music ends in a thundering fortissimo and the spectators are forced to wait for quite some time. At last Löwenstein appears with his blue cap and inspects his army. He ceremonially shakes hands with the commanders and captains while the band plays promenade music. The spectators look on and snigger. When the inspection is over, Lowenstein goes and stands in the middle of the courtyard, tugs at his collar and calls on the ghetto cops to swear obedience to their *Judenältester* (Chairman of the Council of Elders), the *Ältestenrat* (Council of Elders) and to work for the good of Terezín. The brave ghetto police mumble the oath, which is noted with satisfaction by the spectators. Then Eppstein* appears, climbs up on a stool (perhaps this is meant to be symbolic) and delivers a longish speech in which he enumerates the tasks of the *Ghettowache*. In the meantime the important personages carry out their long delayed nose blowing, coughing, pulling up of trousers and such like. The speech finished, the order to march off is given so that the parade itself can be held.

Indeed, a short time later you can hear the marching order being given from the neighboring exit. I nearly faint with surprise because I seem to be watching a regiment of ducks marching by. Strange… seven censored words… and when they appear the entire barracks were laughing, including the ghetto cops who were not in the parade. The Council of Elders watched condescendingly. The music suddenly stopped as if cut off, the ghetto cops lined up to start their march back to barracks, the *Ghettohaus*. Their departure was accompanied with shouts and acclamation unsurpassed by anything I have ever heard. "Do it again!" shouted buoyant children, and the Dresden barracks shook to the foundations.

Since the men in uniform were already far too tired, they did not comply with this request and thus ended this unforgettable farce, the review of the ghetto army.

– Academy (Unknown author)

* Paul Eppstein, second chairman of the Council of Elders of the Terezín ghetto, arrested September 27, 1944 and executed in the Small Fortress of Terezín.

122

Ghetto Cops and Crime Cops

This rabble of vertebrate mammals can be divided into three large groups. First there are the pigs (largely German ghettoites). They are the ones that never, even when given the chance, let their hair down because they are afraid of getting into trouble. The second lot is divided into two groups. The first and larger group are the *Wichtigmacher*, the busybodies. The second and smaller group consists of the yellowbellies who are very diligent in their work and constantly afraid of a German inspection. The third group of ghetto cops and crime cops are referred to as the first-class boys. Unfortunately you don't see them too often, because they form a small minority. They accommodate everyone and, if it is in their power to do so, they help where they can. These are the men that look after our safety. And now I shall tell about meeting one of these men.

"Can I help you?" asked the nurse gruffly of the middle-aged man who had entered the sickroom.

"Secret police, miss," answered the bald gentleman. "I've come to search your premises. A former patient of yours, Pereles, lost a blanket about a month ago and I've been detailed to look for it. The first step in my search will be a thorough inspection of beds and the entire room." I should add that his first step was thorough indeed, because he even looked in my mess kit, just in case the blanket was there.

After the search came the second stage of his investigation: the interrogation, which went like this:

"Who knew what his blanket looked like?"

"I did..." one of the boys called in a loud voice.

"You?"

"... not," said the boy, finishing what he wanted to say.

"Don't you poke fun at the police, you twerp," said the cop. When his efforts did not produce any results, he decided to leave.

At this moment Erik stepped up to him and said politely: "Sir, could you please tell me what your colleagues Sherlock Holmes and Tom Shark are up to?"

"Sorry, I don't know anyone named Sherlock Holmes or Tom Shark. You must be mistaken," replied the detective, and left amidst gales of laughter.

– Pidli (*Emanuel Mühlstein*)

Rambles Through Terezín: An Excursion to the Podmokly Barracks

On Wednesday, November 3 (1943), I decided to have a look into the mysteries surrounding a citizen of Terezín and go to the Podmokly barracks. We began by going to Mrs. Laubová to ask her to sew our stars on firmly. Then we went through our pockets to make sure we had no contraband, and then set out on our merry way. When we got to the barracks my colleague Fischl saw a uniformed man and was so scared he ran about twenty meters. Finally, with God's help, we entered the home of the Terezín dictators – Podmokly.

The yard was in a terrible mess. The Israelites were assiduously pretending to work and walking nonchalantly past the gentlemen from the SS with their hands in their pockets. We entered the spacious hall of the former *Zeughaus* (arsenal), now a furniture warehouse. There we found hundreds of beautiful wardrobes, couches, tables, etc. lying about. Next we went up to the first floor where we saw a cinema under construction.* A lot of people were running about and shouting at each other, for it was supposed to open the following day and wasn't finished yet. When we had had a good look at the beauty of the cinema and all its fixtures we went to the kitchen. There we found many "aryan females" running about in white aprons and white caps (as they do in the ghetto kitchens) busy at the two stoves, making browning for soup. The delightful scent of grilled sausage pervaded the kitchen. In the adjoining room were two boilers where soup and the other courses were being prepared for the entire *Belegschaft*.** Out of interest we mention that the lunch menu consisted of soup, roast potatoes, potato salad and grilled sausage. Partly because our mouths were watering and also because we heard some suspicious shouting outside we left the kitchen, walked quickly through the barracks and outside so that we wouldn't catch hell.

– Fi Be (*probably Herbert Fischl and Beno Kaufmann*)

---

* For the SS.
** Personnel of the Podmokly barracks.

123

Rambles
Through Terezín

The fire station is beyond the wooden houses, between the Magdeburg barracks and the old military riding school. In front of it stands the fire engine and a trailer, and next to it the commandant of the fire brigade, engineer Holzer. Now that would be something to write about, I said to myself, and went straight up to Mr. Holzer to find out everything I could about the fire brigade. Mr. Holzer most willingly started to explain:

– The firemen lead a very strict life here. They must be ready in front of the station at seven o'clock in the morning. Then they do exercises till eight o'clock. At half past eight they start training with their rigs, that is, with the fire engine and extension ladders. Like sacrificial lambs they practice on the barracks or the blocks to improve their agility. At a quarter to ten compulsory schooling begins, and from twelve-thirty on they do various jobs for the benefit of the public. The fact is that when the Technical Department doesn't know how to do a particular job, they send for the fire brigade and let them do it. When a toilet is blocked somewhere, well, what's a fire brigade for?

Checking the blackout is seen to by – who else? The firemen. And first aid? The firemen, of course. The least frequent work we are called upon to do is putting out fires.

Here is a list of their jobs for the last year:
– extinguishing one really large fire;
– extinguishing nine fires caused by electric cables;
– extinguishing a fire in the transformer;
– 29 room fires;
– 14 burning chimneys;
– burning of 330 contaminated mattresses;
– 81 fires on the rubbish dumps;
– work on roofs;
– work for the garrison headquarters;
– sanitary work and many other jobs.

Between May and August, in the women's barracks, we took out 180 sick people and 60 corpses.

Every fireman is equipped with a gas mask, a belt with an axe attached to it, and a helmet. Then there are a few smaller items such as portable fire extinguishers.

The engineer was about to add something when we suddenly heard a voice through the megaphone. He left me and took his place as commander of a group leaving for training, though I'm sure he would have liked to have told me much more.

– nz (*Petr Ginz*)

* This refers to Bedřich Hoffmann, who moved into the home on that day. The "Polish Empire" is an allusion to disparaging comments about the "Polish Jews."

The Great Fire in the Vrchlabí Barracks

At a quarter to eight on Thursday, December 9, I returned as I did every day from the Hannover barracks. When I passed the church I could hear shrill whistling coming from the Vrchlabí barracks. I followed the sound and heard the man with the whistle saying to the *Ghettowachmann: "Grosses Feurer im Hannover!"* (A big fire in the Hannover barracks). I translated that into Czech for my brother as we raced to the scene of the fire.

The fire engine was already there, ready to pump water, but despite the efforts of our volunteer firemen, they couldn't get the engine to pump water. It took about three minutes to get the pump going and then the firemen, standing on the bunker next to the burning wall of the carpenter's shop, started to pump water through the window into the burning rooms. A strong spotlight illuminated the scene. After a little while steam and smoke began to rise so that we could not see anything. But then the Ghettowache came and cleared the area. We were forced to leave and so my report is finished.

– Paintbrush (*Unknown author*)

News from the Terezín Press Agency

On February 1, Camp Commandant Burger left our ghetto and was replaced by Rahm, who comes from Mother Prague. Burger's departure and Rahm's arrival meant that, as far as we were concerned, conditions in our camp changed for the better. The first order Rahm issued during a walk through Terezín was that the square should be turned into a park. In the center would be a pavilion and every evening a band in uniform would play for the inhabitants of Terezín. Another news report concerned Jews from mixed marriages whose Aryan mothers or fathers were living outside the ghetto. These Aryan relatives – so the report went – would be allowed ten-minute visits at the garrison headquarters. Every interview would be supervised by a German soldier.

The next items concern our home. The first report is sad, but we are men and will take it like men. Fritz Hoffmann was exiled from the Polish Empire. The Polish Embassy issued him a passport to the Republic of Shkid. This transfer occurred on February 11, 1944.*

Zdeněk Taussig is to join our Home within the next few days. Let us hope that his arrival will see an increase in the sporting spirit in our home.

I would also like to report that miracles still happen. Our beloved Jirka Bruml didn't spill a single drop from the wash basin. Nothing like it has occurred in our sixty weeks of self-government.

This ends my broadcast. I will now switch you to Radio Cuckoo Land.

– Nácek (*Unknown author*)

125

Bedřich Hoffmann
(b. 1932, perished).
"Landscape with House."
Aquarelle, pencil,
320 × 205 mm.
Jewish Museum, Prague,
Inv. No. 130742.

Sensation, Sensation!!

According to the Jewish *Bonkes* Radio* a Swedish Commission is to visit the capital of the Jewish reservation, Theresienstadt. On December 6, the center of Jews in Bohemia will be visited by several dignitaries from higher up. The following details have been announced: First of all, on the day of the visit a large bun and unlimited quantities of coffee with milk and sugar are to be issued during the morning. There will be something for the old and sick, a double portion of meat and potatoes for lunch, and in the evening, dumplings with sweet sauce.

Secondly, the Garrison Headquarters have ordered an intensive *Verschönerungsaktion.***

Thirdly, on the day of arrival perfect order must be maintained from half-past eight onwards. For this purpose permission has been given to air, shake out and beat comforters, blankets, mattresses, etc. throughout the preceding day.

December 5, 1943. According to the proverb "Don't do today what you can put off till tomorrow," all the preparations are being made at the last minute. The *Strassenreinigung**** are running about scared in the streets, the *Hundertschaft***** is painting fences with a reddish-brownish-blackish paint most pleasing to the eye, the window dressers are putting new displays in the windows, the youth leaders are chasing round the Homes, little old ladies are scurrying through the streets in search of somebody they could entrust some new *bonkes* to, or to argue with. In the shop window of the *Damenbekleidung* (ladies' clothing shop) there is a beautiful paper menorah with the inscription "Hanukkah 5704" (there should really be an explanation of what Hanukkah is for the Swedish Commission), while in the shop window of the *Herrenbekleidung* (gentlemen's clothing shop) there are pictures with captions describing in detail Mr. X's shopping trip to the store. (It should be pointed out that he arrived stark naked, covered only with a piece from a straw tick, with clothing coupons and money, and that he departed the perfect image of a Terezín fop.) In the shop window for kitchen utensils there is a multitude of containers with inscriptions in Czech: rice, semolina, bread crumbs, poppy seed, etc., all of them entirely inaccessible to the likes of us.

On December 6, 1943, we must again begin with a proverb: "Man proposes and the food supply department disposes," because for breakfast, instead of the expected sweet bun and coffee with milk and sugar there was only real hot black Melta ersatz coffee. The morning passed in high expectations, but that was all they gave us. At lunch we had the favorite food of the Israelite nation since the days of Moses' in the desert – barley manna. After lunch tension reached its peak. But the Swedish Commission was evidently keeping us waiting. A certain boy from L 417, seeing that there would be no visitors, declared sulkily, "I needn't have washed last night!"

But we won't waste readers' time any

* Rumor Radio.
** Beautification drive before the arrival of the International Red Cross Commission.
*** Working crew responsible for cleanliness in the streets.
**** Working commandos.

* Soup made from extract.
** This refers to Rahm,
   the last commandant
   of Terezín.

longer with details. It must be added, how-ever, that to everybody's disappointment the Commission did not show up, and for supper the soup was only *Extraktsuppe*.* And so I end my reportage, and let us hope that we shall not be put to shame.

P.S. The expected party arrived on the 7th, and filled their faces at the Victoria restaurant.

(Hanuš Weil and František Feuerstein)

Terezín – the Future Spa

In the night between the 10th and 11th of April I crept into the minds of the Terezín *bonkes* men, to find out what Father Bedřich** intends to do for the autonomous republic. The first thing I learned was that our Father intends to issue an order the gist of which is that all work squads will be forced to send their youngest personnel to do so-called maintenance work. To assure the rapid reconstruction of our town, it was our Father's wish that specialists of all kinds should participate to the fullest extent. For this purpose Father Bedřich had the gymnasium, which had been turned into a hospital, cleared to have it converted into a synagogue, theater, and future cinema. According to the latest news, which I obtained just a few hours before writing this, an open-air cafe is to be established on the roof of the gymnasium. He had the barbed-wire fence on the square removed and the square transformed into a park, where he had a music pavilion erected to give the inhabitants of Terezín an opportunity for entertainment and refreshment during their lunch hour and in the evening after work.

One fine day, when Father Bedřich inspected our town, he did not like the walls separating the various houses in Terezín, be-

127

cause he thought they disrupted the beauty of the town. He called the mayor of this free town of ours on the carpet and ordered him to make these walls disappear within forty-eight hours. To ensure a plentiful supply of mineral water for the town, he had a well dug beyond the outskirts. At this point, a depth of 80 meters has been reached, without yet finding a trace of water. A restaurant is also to be established in the park on the square. It has not been settled yet what is to be sold there. A number of horse-drawn carriages have been ordered by the town council for our world-class spa. The working population of Terezín will also be well served. A trolley-bus network is to be established to make going and coming to work easier. And when checking on the city homes for young people Father Bedřich issued an order to have them all renovated in the shortest possible time.

Since our dear Father wanted to be able to check up on his children while they worked, he set new working hours. That is the latest news I've been able to extract from the brains of our *bonkes* men. Part of these regulations have already been put into practice and let us hope that our *bonkes* men were right about the other reports as well. And we wish to express our thanks to Father Bedřich for working to improve our well being.

– Sydicus (*Unknown author*)

This is Not a Gang, or Making a Movie in Our Town (A Comedy in Three Acts)

"I am told the Jews in Terezín are not feeling too well," said the director of the Department of Jewish Problems to his assistant one fine day. "And what is more," he continued indignantly, "I hear that reports have been appearing in the foreign press about the wretched state of these Jews. This can't go on. It could become an international scandal and it will make things quite impossible for us, not to mention our people on the spot. You know how it is."

"But what steps would you like to take to counteract this? After all, we can't possibly give them more food or improve their living conditions. That would be against our anti-Semitic principles."

"Hm, a difficult problem," replied Mr. X regretfully, "but I don't think there's anything else we can do."

"Wait a minute – yes, that's it! We'll make a movie (surely you must know something about trick films) and we'll send copies to all these inquisitive countries that are sticking their noses into what does not concern them."

"I've always said I had an first-class assistant. I shall recommend a promotion for you, and a medal for your clearheaded ideas."

That was the prologue.

And then matters proceeded very quickly.

Newsreel directors Pečenka, Frič, etc. "Now then, gentlemen, you with the long nose, you Fatso, you four-eyes, line up for filming. Look pleasant, satisfied, as if you'd just dined on goose. What, you stinking Jew, what sort of a look is that? Here's a slap in the face for you" – and the blows begin to fall, elbow jabs, kicks administered by a gentleman in green to the head of a helpless old man. A whole company of old ladies are commandeered to go and bathe. "Please I can't, I have diarrhea, rheumatism..." *"Halt Maul, alte Jüdin, gehst ins Wasser."* An old lady, who doesn't even know how to swim, has to get into the water.

The next part of this valuable film:

Orthodox Jews and rabbis were sent to the *Stadtkapelle** and had to jump up and down to the rhythm of the jazz band. Oh, and the food! The Jews lick their chops after devouring the excellent cakes and sweet buns

* Municipal orchestra, set up for the Nazi propaganda film.

* Children's pavilion, set
 up for the Nazi
 propaganda film.
** The "Bank of the
 Jewish Self-
 Government" was built
 for the Nazi
 propaganda film.
*** Coffee-house built for
 the Nazi propaganda
 film.

(naturally, only when the camera is pointing at them) and afterwards they practically pumped their stomachs out. The best cabarets, the *Kinderpavillon** – everything was filmed, and filmed, of course, "with a natural smile on the lips."

That was the intermezzo.

This movie business was an excellent idea, sir... You see, we did it without magnifying mirrors, without improving their living conditions, and now we are redeemed in the eyes of our friendly enemies.

And that was the conclusion.

– Don (*Herbert Fischl*)

Without Title

Terezín has now really become a miniature state with a slightly limited autonomy. Partly it is a movie lot – what else is *Die Bank der jüdischen Selbstverwaltung*** for, with its ostentatious plaque announcing that you can make and withdraw deposits, open current accounts and similar swindles. There are department stores with elegant window displays, though the interior and staff are less elegant. And finally, a town with an area of not quite one square kilometer is divided into four administrative districts and abounds in government offices. The minister of the interior... (censored)... We have our own plainclothes police. And as you surely know all of this is only on the order from above. Which social category can we be compared to? Prisoners of war? An international convention was set up for them, but not for us... (Unfinished, for the reason mentioned above.)

– Academy (*Unknown author*)

View from the Coffee House***

Oh, the coffee house is a wonderful place,
They've got tea and coffee and air and space,
But the music's off-key, and I look down
On the German HQ in the garrison town.
And the wenches that carry the coffee in
Wear their faces bent in a permanent grin.

I'm having fun too, and my face is smiling
(While down below they cart off the dying
And old men are pushing the funeral carts
With tears in their eyes and heavy hearts.)
And that green building, its outlines vague
Is left half empty by a typhoid plague.

Why must we sit here, void of strife
While the "world down there" fights for its life?
People clap hands while the band plays jazz,
And I'm carried away by the razzamatazz
That assaults my ear like a caterwauling,
Like ravens in winter, raucous, appalling,
Like shattering glass, like a cresting wave
That would fling me ashore and into my grave.

I embrace it, this world of time and tide,
The world where anguish and hunger collide.
Like sun-kissed blossoms winding round me,
It welcomes me back to reality.

– Ha- (*Hanuš Hachenburg*)

Would you care for dessert?

A clean tablecloth, tasteful tables –
Gentlemen in dark suits –
Girls painted scarlet –
Witty repartee –
Swinging jazz –
Coffee served in the salon –
You can even get whipped cream –
Or just get whipped – but that's next door.*

(*Josef Taussig*)**

* "Next door" to the coffee house were the headquarters of the German garrison where prisoners were interrogated.

** Josef Taussig (1914 to 1945) was a journalist, publicist, and writer. In 1942 he was deported to Terezín, where he went on with his literary work illegally. A frequent guest of "Home Number One" in L 417, he was deported in 1944 to Auschwitz, and in 1945 to Gross Rosen and Flossenburg, where he died.

*** "Degeneration" refers to the years 1942–1943, when the prisoners of Terezín had to "acknowledge" the SS men and all persons in uniform. The men had to raise their caps and the women had to bow deeply. In 1944, when a visit from the International Red Cross was expected, "acknowledging" was strictly prohibited.

Satirical verses appeared also in *Vedem* under the title "A Small Guide Through Terezín."

VEDEM, Terezín 1943
Degeneration***

In the temple of Apis
– so history tells us –
The ancient Egyptians
Saluted the bull.
This cult declined
over the course of time.
Today we raise our hats to nearly any… (idiot).

(*Josef Taussig*)

* Schleuse (from the German, "floodgate" or "lock") was the name of the place where transports arrived and departed. People called up to be transported always tried to wear what they had not been able to include in the fifty-kilogram luggage limit.

VEDEM, Terezín 1943

The Happy Father

Devil take all these transports,
How they made us sweat.
And what luck that our boy
Was in bed with pneumonia.

(*Josef Taussig*)

VEDEM, Terezín 1942–1944

Love in the Floodgates*

My darling, I'd love to kiss you so
But you're all wrapped up from head to toe.
Five panties, two dresses, a cap and a hat,
How can a chap get his arms around that?

(*Josef Taussig*)

Erika Stránská
(b. 1930, perished).
Collage, 250 × 175 mm.
Jewish Museum, Prague,
Inv. No. 131942.

Folk Songs from Terezín

(These are new lyrics for old folk songs, written by Valtr Eisinger.)

Sonny boy, sonny boy, are you at home?
The Arbeitsamt's asking where you did roam?
I've been slaving away, but it's never enough
Been working so hard that I'm ready to snuff.

I'm just a little cook
I can barely hold a book,
But when there's dumplings for lunch
I can carry a bunch.

Just wait, I'm going to tell on you
You've been scavenging again, you know it's true;
Dumplings from the scullery,
Bread from the bakery
Just wait, I'm going to tell on you.

A ghetto cop stands watch both day and night
His badge upon his coat is in plain sight
And while the wind is blowing he gets booty
Cadging cigarettes while he's on duty.

Tra-rah boomty aye
No electric lights today.
Tra-rah boomty aye
There'll be no light today.

When I was going to Ústí
To watch the transports leave
I used to scavenge what I could
For fun, and out of need.

Flow on, thou waters, from the tap
The Wasserdienst* checks out the sink;
But when you really need the stuff
There's n'er a drop to drink.

* The ghetto water service crew.

The carpenters built us a big latrine
The cooks stir our grub in a big tureen
The grub passes through us, and we thank our stars
We sit there for hours on the carpenters' dream…

Here comes the mailman, bringing the mail
Parcels for the big shots, without fail.
There goes the mailman, walk the other way
Never brings us nothing but the time of day.

I come from Kutná Hora
A retrained cobbler am I.
I used to run a big bank
Now that was something fine!
But when they come and ask me
What I would rather choose
I tell them, "Boys, there's nothing
Like making a pair of shoes."

I'm a cop and a cop I'll be
Truncheon in my hand for you to see
I got the truncheon from Litowitz
But I haven't a clue what to do with it.

Eneky beneky here come the cops
Abracadabra let's shut up
Holus bolus kickety poo
We're going to jail whatever we do.

Collected, from among the people, by -nger (*Valtr Eisinger*).

Officialdom in the
Magdeburg Barracks

"Moving out?" Impossible!
What did you say your name was?
What? You're Sigismund Edelstein?*
HIS cousin's granddad?
Why didn't you say so in the first place?
Here's your Übersiedlungsschein!**

(*Josef Taussig*)

Summer is a-coming in
No shirt have I to wear.
Thank God my chum in the clothing store
Will find me something there.

When man progressed to artificial light
He said "Let there be darkness"
And introduced *Lichtsperre*.***

– Academy (*Unknown author*)

Mey fah zu, or:
The Indolence
of the Manchus

A country lane leads through wet, muddy
Manchuria. The deep cart tracks indicate
long use. Every now and then our car stops
and we have to get out and push our Tatra
out of the ruts. We slam it in gear and continue at a snail's pace. The car lurches over
potholes and through puddles. At last a half
derelict hut appears and a Manchu emerges.
We stop and climb out of the car. We see
a Manchu village. Soon the entire family sur-
rounds us. We have breakfast. I turn to the
young Manchu. "For heaven's sake, man,

* The epigram uses the
family name of the first
chairman of the
"Council of Elders" of
Terezín, Jacob
Edelstein (arrested
November 9, 1943, and
transported to
Auschwitz where he
was shot on June 30,
1944, together with his
wife and son).
** Emigration papers.
*** Blackout.

why don't you repair the road? It's almost impassable."

"Mey fah zu," answers the Manchu, "It can't be helped."

That is the general opinion in Manchuria. Although the road was being used daily, no one even dreamed of repairing it. The road is a mess? So it's a mess. Mey fah zu, it can't be helped. And if you think I'm only concerned with Manchu philosophy, let me tell you: Manchuria is not the only place where there are Manchus. There are plenty of them here, too. Are we in Terezín? Mey fah zu. Are we sweating like pigs? Mey fah zu. Favoritism at every step? Mey fah zu. They take everything as given, unpleasant to be sure, but unchangeable. Is there favoritism here? Can't be helped. Favoritism is as immutable, as natural as the rotation of the earth or gravitation. It was so in the past, it will be so again. Mey fah zu.

Don't let your mind be blunted by Terezín! Don't stare at things like cattle. Fight against every injustice. Death to the Manchus!

– Academy (*Petr Ginz*)

The song

Hey ho, the ship sails over the sea.
Happily in the wind the sail is filling.
Ahoy, pirate, your time has come
Ahoy, pirate, draw your cutlass!

Hey, ho and a bottle of rum.

A ship approaches, unawares.
Sailors are singing in the rigging.
Now they've seen us, now she's running
The masts groan, the stitching bursts,

Hey, ho, and a bottle of rum

But all their efforts are in vain
Our vessel closes in upon them;
Grapples them to her, all draw their knives
And all set to in savage battle.

Hey ho, and a bottle of rum

We pirates – oh, we are the best!
We vanquished a ship upon the sea.
We have a barrel full of gold.
The ship now sinks, her dead aboard.

Hey, ho and a bottle of rum.

Psychology
of the Masses

This title – perhaps for the first time – is not intended to introduce theories, correct or otherwise, on the modes, types, and distinguishing features of mass psychology, whether that mass contains ten, a hundred, or a thousand or more individuals. I would like only to show (and I strongly doubt that I shall succeed) how I was affected by the psychosis and mood of a specific mob, how they evoked feelings that will have a lasting impact on me. (You must have guessed by now that I refer to the departure from the Bohušovice valley on Thursday, November 11.)

On the morning of the Thursday I got up and was looking forward to enjoying the whole day. I was in an excellent mood. I was making jokes about decimation, being sent to Poland, being shot, etc. – about whatever the fantasy of our Terezín *bonkes* men could come up with. Then I fell in line, my feet were cold and it all seemed terribly funny: how slowly we were moving forward, how the mothers pushed their *Kriechlinge** wrapped in heaven knows what and on top of that, in an eiderdown, a blanket, and a pillow, in those caricatures of prams that are mostly laundry baskets on wooden wheels.

Then we reached our destination, and even the white crematorium looked ridiculous, like a silo. Then I stopped and stood still.

Evening. Will we be here all night? It is getting dark, people are pushing towards the exit, whispering to each other. The sick are fainting. At first I only wonder about it, but then I become convinced that a single shout of "Forward everybody!" would bring about an unexpected catastrophe. It's like a powder barrel ready to explode.

Had we stayed there all night, such a catastrophe would indeed have occurred. The sick would have trampled each other down, yelled, stormed the barriers, got back to the ghetto and settled down in their blocks.

I started to hum the Marseillaise. "I can't stand this," said Benošek, "stop it!" I stopped singing. People pressed toward the exit, and were driven back by the gendarmes; others pushed forward again. The crowd behaved like water when it starts to boil and just before it boils over. Then the order to depart came. I was terrified of getting lost among all those egoists, forty thousand of them, because getting lost in such a throng would have depressed me terribly. People pushed. Forty thousand rushed toward the exit and as Aaron and I could see, were held back only by the bayonets. I was somewhat relieved by the wooden building in front of me. It was something solid to hang onto, because the crowd that was practically trampling over each other was, after all, like waves on a sea in which it was only too easy to drown. The slogan was: Get home! It was useless to call out: "For heaven's sake, people, don't push, you'll crush yourselves to death!" "Women and children first!" or "Help the old people!"

Eventually I managed to get home. I was neither the first nor the last. I pushed, because the others were pushing, and I made it through. That is all. Not surprising, given what I've just described, that one mother's pram with the baby in it was smashed, many people fainted or threw hysterical fits. I am not taking away from yesterday's events a great social theory, merely a great social experience.

– Ha- (*Hanuš Hachenburg*)

* Toddlers.

136

Editorial

"Loonie" and "idiot" are the most frequently used terms in the vocabulary of Terezín boys. Lentil soup, youth leader, the hot weather, today's football match, Madrich, the evening program, liver pate – everything is idiotic. The term loonie is applied to all the above mentioned human beings, including friends, siblings, mothers, and fathers. There is no hypocrisy here: the nine- or fifteen-year-old inhabitant of L 417 will calmly call his friend an idiot. The statement that a proposal, the Madrich's order, a book written by an Olbracht, a Hostovský, a Poláček, is idiotic, is pronounced in a loud voice, with such certainty and matter-of-factness that it is persuasive.

You get used to these two words, and sooner or later they become part of your vocabulary too, along with a number of other Terezín slang words that we shall discuss elsewhere.

Loonie and idiot. But there comes suddenly a sobering-up. You pass a building where faces old and young are pressed against barred windows – loonies. These pale and terrified faces have a common feature; I can't quite express it – strange faces, but there is one I know and it recognizes me. An older woman starts to laugh hysterically. Her front teeth are missing, she drools disgustingly. She hisses at me, I approach the window, she leans forward and passes me a crumpled, filthy piece of paper. Buy my slippers, buy my slippers, the woman offers in a desperate voice, the woman in whom I have recognized the mother of one of the boys from L 417. Four months ago she was a young, thirty-five-year-old woman, today she is old, gray-haired, toothless. "I'm starving, I'm starving, buy my slippers ..." she pleads, quite hoarse by now. But all I could hear at that moment was the clear, boyish voice of her son, a hundred strong, young voices, crying, "Loonie, Loonie!"

Boys, do you realize that every word has its meaning? You don't refer to tall people as giants, to toddlers as dwarfs, to blond heads as canaries, to brunets as Schwarters. If you did, they would regard you as – LOONIES!

Boys, respect your comrades, respect yourselves. You are responsible not only for your actions, but also for your words. Every one of your mothers may one day have to sell slippers made of crumpled paper from behind the barred windows of the madhouse.

– Pepek (*Josef Stiassny*)

Slogan of the Day: The Young Help the Aged

Do you still remember the time when, in Prague or Brno, you got up to offer your seat in the tram to an old man, when your mother bent down to pick up a parcel, or an umbrella dropped from the trembling hands of an old woman? We live in Terezín, the town of the floodgate and the black market, a town where the stronger triumph over the weaker, in a ghetto shaped by primitive urges, by the fight for an extra ration, a place in the line for bread, in front of the distribution center for clothes and shoes, in the dentist's office. Respect for age, once personified in the beautiful white hair of your grandmother, your mother's mother, has disappeared. Today, old age is personified by the aged from Vienna, Berlin, Cologne, hundreds, thousands of strange, starving, sick people who need looking after, and who stand before you.

The aged from the Protectorate were transported in cattle wagons to the east, that they might never (do you realize the terror of that word?) ever again see their children, their grandchildren.

Several old men and women from Germany live in Terezín today. They not only live in the ghetto, they live in a strange and, let's be honest, hostile environment. Hunger, terrible living conditions, illness and homesickness have caused bitterness, nervousness, mistrust, and a strong tendency to quarrel among these aged from Germany. Age is not taboo for us. We are not, and shall never be, in favor of injections that artificially prolong life or hasten dying.

Somewhere in Poland the old, sick, starving, abandoned mother of your mother remembers. Let us regard them with the affectionate look of our childhood, let us refresh them with our youthful smile, let us support them with the strength of our manhood – the aged from Germany, the sick, the starving, the abandoned.

– Pepek (*Josef Stiassny*)

Marie: What position did the author of those amazing editorials, Josef Stiassny, hold in your home?

Kurt: If Valtr Eisinger was the personification of authority and the strict teacher, without whom daily life in our home in "Number One" would have been unimaginable, then I remember Pepek Stiassny above all as a very dear person and an understanding friend.

Zdeněk: Pepek was Eisinger's assistant. He was awfully tall, and his height was exaggerated by his extreme thinness. He was almost pathologically honest. He could never manage to get himself something by some less-than-honest means, though this sort of thing was quite acceptable in Terezín, so he was dependent completely on the meager Terezín rations, and he often gave away some of the little he got.

Kurt: We were all very fond of Pepek. He wrote fascinating articles for the magazine, and he was an outstanding storyteller. We trusted him completely. For instance, we would confide in him whenever we had problems typical for kids our age, problems connected with growing up. And Pepek knew how to answer our questions. He would talk quite openly, for example, about relationships between men and women, about anything.

Zdeněk: And not only that, in this crowded milieu, he could create an atmosphere of domestic intimacy. He would always gather two or three boys around him and talk to them about various problems. He was never forceful, but he always managed to intervene wherever it was necessary.

Josef Stiassny was born on September 16, 1916. He spent his childhood in Německý Brod. It was only after his father's death that his mother moved to Prague with her four children. Josef Stiassny's brother Petr was arrested early in the German occupation for taking part in the Resistance, and was executed. The only one of the family to survive was Pepek's elder sister, Dr. Gertruda Sekaninová-Čakrtová.* In conversation with her, she confirmed everything that Pepek Stiassny's wards in "Number One" said about him. She gave me the addresses of Pepek's friends and told me that the writer Norbert Frýd had mentioned Pepek in his books about the war.

Mr. Jaroslav Kuna was in daily touch with Pepek in 1937 and 1938. They were both training to be booksellers and were not only schoolmates, but close colleagues.

At that time there was a magazine called *Booksellers' Survey* and Jaroslav Kuna, along with Pepek Stiassny and some other young people, published a supplement entitled "The Young Bookseller." Pepek Stiassny was in charge of the cultural column "Culture for Trainees." This column, and indeed "The Young Bookseller," focused on everything that was progressive in our pre-war culture. Pepek Stiassny himself wrote many of the reviews and also some short theoretical articles, often under the name of Pavel Glücklich. Some letters addressed to Jaroslav Kuna date back to this time and are proof of how enthusiastically Pepek worked for "The Young Bookseller."

* Dr. Gertruda Sekaninová-Čakrtová (1908–1986), a lawyer, survived Terezín, Auschwitz, and Gross-Rosen concentration camps. From 1949 till 1957 she was Deputy Minister of Foreign Affairs. In 1968 she was one of four members of parliament who voted against the Soviet aggression against Czechoslovakia. In 1977 she signed the human rights initiative "Charter 77." She chaired the Committee for the Defense of the Unjustly Prosecuted.

Hana Kohnová
(b. 1931, perished).
Aquarelle, 285 × 210 mm.
Jewish Museum, Prague,
Inv. No. 129917.

Mr. Ivan Zmatlík was a frequent visitor at the Stiassnys, where many young people met for lively discussions, even after the outbreak of war. At that time Pepek greatly admired Helena Fantlová, the wife of his friend, the young poet Hanuš Fantl, both of whom were frequent guests in the Stiassny household. This secret passion caused Pepek a great deal of suffering. He even moved away from home and found lodgings on his own. He carefully guarded his privacy, but would invite Ivan Zmatlík to his room.

It was a bare room, almost without furniture. There was a bed of sorts, and a chair, and what especially caught the eye was a reproduction of Van Gogh's "Night Cafe." Pepek had a special relationship with this picture. When he got his summons for Terezín (he joined the transport of July 27, 1942) he cut the reproduction into pieces, glued them on a piece of canvas so it could be folded like a map, and thereafter he always carried it with him. "The Night Cafe" must have gone with him on his last journey to Auschwitz.

Pepek's friend Hanuš Fantl was arrested in October, 1941, for active participation in the Resistance movement, and sent to the concentration camp of Mauthausen. His wife was arrested with him. She was later released from the Ravensbrück concentration camp. Her daughter Jana was born in Prague and was barely three months old when she and her mother were taken to Terezín. Hanuš Fantl was shot in Mauthausen on March 18, 1942. Pepek looked after Helena Fantlová and little Jana not only in Prague, but throughout his stay in Terezín, until September 28, 1944, when he was taken to Auschwitz. He made it through the selection process but ended his life soon afterwards by running against the electrified wires surrounding the camp. Helena Fantlová and her daughter perished in the gas chambers of Auschwitz in October, 1944.

Motto of the Week:
Why? Because!

A few days ago, somebody said to me as darkness fell that Terezín was like a bad dream. For a young person, Terezín is and must be a time of life when he can gain the experience of a decade, for here one has the chance to test any theory in practice within a few minutes. Terezín is the world in a nutshell. Here you can look behind the scenes of the world stage in miniature. You see the actors without their masks, you are actor and onlooker in one, you watch the drama even as you live through it.

But Terezín is not the world. The world is outside the barbed wire separating this ghetto, this city of passivity, from the world that is fighting for ideals, the world of activity. In the lives of our young people, Terezín must remain a mere episode, but it is here that we must learn to face reality, life and death, logically, critically, manfully!

Boys, perhaps in a few years' time a woman who lived for months in the ghetto of Terezín and has seen so much moral and physical filth, the starvation of older women, the despair of young mothers whose babies are dying – this woman may scream hysterically when a tiny gray mouse runs out from under her cupboard.

Perhaps, in a few years' time, you will meet a man who worked in the Terezín *Transportleitung*, dispatching transports to the east and receiving transports of old, dying and dead German Jews at the station of Bohušovice, and he will be waxing sentimental and maudlin over the fate of some screen lovers.

That man and woman lived in Terezín, but they never asked themselves the question: "Why?" And if they did ask it, they didn't come up with the right answer, they didn't go to the root of the matter. For them, Terezín was the world and they were the center of this world, I (Josef Kohn), WE (the Jews, the Jewish question).

Friends, let us ask today and tomorrow WHY, and let each of us answer this "why" with a clear, logical THIS IS WHY! If we do this, there will not be one woman amongst us spreading rumors, there will not be any crybabies amongst us – boys with their hands folded in their laps, shamefully weeping bitter tears over the misery of our collective fate – the Jewish existence. There will be real boys – men who have not inscribed "Prayer" on their escutcheon, but "Action," fighters who believe in ideals, and are for actively fighting for those ideals.

– Pepek (*Josef Stiassny*)

Gerti Kleinová
(b. 1930, survived).
Collage, 250 × 200 mm.
Jewish Museum, Prague,
Inv. No. 133430.

* The military riding school.

District Heating

Work in Terezín is impeded by the fact that there are insufficient tools. But against all expectation, considering that there is a war on, there is more building material inside the ghetto than outside. And since there is sufficient material, many large construction works are under way. One of them is the district heating system. I should like to give you a brief report on this matter.

The central boiler room is in the brewery. Of two boilers, only one is so far in operation. The second will be ready in a month. The boilers are fired up day and night. There are three shifts of stokers. In the course of twenty-four hours, 80 to 100 metric units of coal dust are burnt. Coal dust can be used thanks to a forced air system that drives air under the thick grate. From the boilers, the steam goes to a distributor, and from there it goes toward the Kavalír barracks. There is a branch pipeline to the disinfection baths, to the Central Bath and to the delousing bath. In the kitchen the high-pressure steam (8 atm, 60 degrees C) is reduced to low pressure (0.4 atm) and from there into boilers that release only water, retaining the steam. From the boilers the condensation flows into a reservoir, where it is pumped into the underground shafts beneath the brewery. From L 408, the condensation flows underground back into the brewery. Now steam heating is also under construction in the Reitschule.* In the brewery boiler room there is a water softening installation, because otherwise sediment would form in the boiler due to the hard water.

That is the end of my report. I hope you have understood everything.

– Bear Brady (*George Brady*)

Questions and Answers

What good to mankind is the beauty of science?
What good is the beauty of pretty girls?
What good is a world when there are no rights?
What good is the sun when there is no day?
What good is God? Is he only to punish?
Or to make life better for mankind?
Or are we beasts, vainly to suffer
And rot beneath the yoke of our feelings?

What good is life, when the living suffer?
Why is my world surrounded by walls?
Know son, this is here for a reason:
To make you fight and conquer all!

– Ha- (*Hanuš Hachenburg*)

142

The Ramparts

The ramparts, the playing fields of Terezín. When I first came to the ramparts, the so-called playing field was a sad sight. It was a piece of lumpy ground where a group of youngsters were working to level it. Since then much time has passed. One day a rumor made the rounds of the school that we were going to rehearse a play to celebrate the opening of the ramparts; and hardly had this rumor gone through L 417, when another came: there would be an assembly* of all young people on the ramparts, where the playing field would be ceremonially handed over.

Full of curiosity, I went to have a look at the ramparts, and was met with the sight of a lovely playing field with two goals. It was the work of our comrades, who did it not only for us, but for the entire population of Terezín. What I have described here is only a small illustration of the fact that when the grown-ups say that the young people in Terezín only learn to steal, they are very wrong indeed. They are certainly learning one thing here: to appreciate physical labor.

– Švejk (*Hanuš Kominík*)

Rambles
Through Terezín

A room in the entrails of the Kavalír barracks** with the stink of the latrines, bad light, physical and mental muck. The only worry is to eat one's fill, to sleep enough and …? What more? An intellectual life? Can anything else exist in these underground burrows but a mere animal instinct to satisfy bodily needs? And yet it is possible! The seed of creative thought does not perish in mud and mire. Even there, it sprouts and blossoms like a star shining in the dark.

This is exemplified by the blind artist Berthold Ordner. One day Jiříček Schubert and I went to see him so that I could write about him for our magazine. We quickly introduced ourselves and then I asked him to tell me something about himself. Unfortunately he spoke German so that I did not understand him too well.

"Ever since I was young," he told us, "I was receptive to anything occurring before my eyes. When my blindness came, I had to give up drawing. I could not see what I was drawing, nor could I feel and touch it. In short, I lacked the third dimension. So I turned to wire." And with these words, he took from his shelf a wonderful peacock made of thin brass wire. I could not admire the beautiful lines and the workmanship of the piece enough. The eyes on the peacock's tail were fashioned from a piece of wire twisted into a spiral.

"How do you go about your work?" I asked.

"I first shape the frame, and when it seems right to me I work out the details, the muscles, etc., with thin wire."

"How can you remember the shapes of your subjects so accurately after not having seen them for more than twenty-five years?"

"It's only thanks to memory. I can recall the objects I saw in my youth and now, twenty years later, I shape them as I understood them at the time. It is a method similar to what the expressionists use. Look at a house, then fashion it mainly in terms of its contours and shape. Colors are of secondary importance. This is what I do, only the interval between observing the model and recreating it is somewhat longer. Twenty-five years! So much has changed in the meantime! I used to exhibit my works in America, France, Great Britain, Germany, Spain, Sweden, and elsewhere. Museums fought over my creations. And now here in Terezín I suffer

Berthold Ordner, the blind Austrian artist (b. 1889, survived). Three wire figurines: "The Standard Bearer," "Horse," "Elephant," and a photographic portrait of the artist. (The photographs probably date from before the artist's deportation from Vienna to the Ghetto, where he continued his creative work using scraps of wire.) Memorial of Terezín, *Vedem* pp. 102, 103.

from hunger, I haven't enough wire to work."

"Do you still mind being blind?" I asked him.

"Sometimes, when I am thinking, I do not miss my sight at all. At such moments, in my mind, I leave the filth here completely behind. These are my happiest moments."

I looked at him in admiration. But then Jiříček the Joker glanced at his watch and realized with terror that it was already eight o'clock. We quickly took our leave of the blind artist (he promised to look us up sometime) and hurried out. We welcomed the fresh air after the fusty atmosphere in the depth of the Kavalír barracks and soon we safely reached our Home.

– nz (*Petr Ginz*)

nity he would come and see us again and demonstrate how to create little figures from wire. His lecture was surely one of the best and most interesting ever held in Home Number One.

– Durodka Macháček (*Leoš Marody*)

Cultural Report

Thanks to Jiříček the Joker the blind artist Mr. Berthold Ordner... came to see us on Saturday the 3rd of this month. He brought a few samples of his art. It is really admirable that a man who lost his sight twenty-five years ago manages to remember the shape of animals and people and to model them so accurately and faithfully in wire. Boys from other homes, and even their parents, attended the lecture. Mr. Ordner spoke German but even so everybody understood him, for he spoke slowly and clearly.

He promised us that at the next opportu-

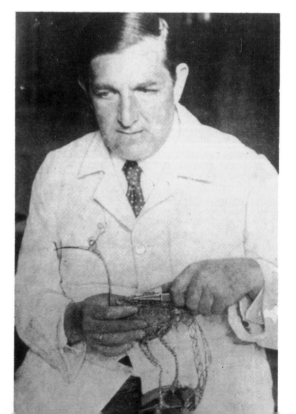

You gray steel clouds, driven by the wind
Hurrying to unknown destinations
Carrying within you the image of blue skies
Carrying within you ash-gray smoke
Carrying within you the blood-red phantom of strife
You, gray clouds, protect us! You that are only vapor
You, sailing through the worlds, driven by the winds
Like the eternal pilgrim waiting for his death.
I want one day, like you, to cover distances
Far into the future, never to return.
You, ashen clouds on the horizon
Forever our hope and our symbol
You, whose tempest can veil the sun
You, driven by time, but followed by day!

– Hachenburg (*Hanuš Hachenburg*)

The Madman

I walk the streets alone and alone
Pondering the evil in the world.
And thoughts about it fill my mind,
As I walk the dark streets
alone and alone.
I remember. Long, long ago,
A madman wished to change the world,
Turn it upside down and inside out,
Fill people and youth with one ideal:
Take nothing on trust, let nothing stand,
Fight for every inch of land.
If something is down, then lift it up,
If others stay silent, you must speak up.
And so this madman years ago
Tried turning the world upside down
And walked his cat instead of his dog.

– Ca – nz (*Petr Ginz*)

Long Live Life

I want to give you a brief picture of how Švenk's play "Long Live Life" came about. There were many rehearsals, and then it came time for the dress rehearsal. It was to be held on March 24 in the Magdeburg barracks. I arranged to meet Pepek, Leoš, and Jiříček. We arrived for the rehearsal at ten and they only let us in at ten-thirty. There were about a hundred people there all wanting to watch. Nothing was ready and so we had to start setting up the props. Every participant had to work, to help, change into costumes, etc. Then Švenk had to point out several times that people who weren't in it had no business being there, but nobody wanted to leave, so they threw Pepek and the others out. Then the rehearsal began. Things went quite well. There was great excitement and some of the scenes had to be done over again. The rehearsal finished at half past three in the morning and then we had to listen to criticism. Then the tickets for the first night were handed out.

The long awaited day of the premiere came. The play was successful.

At the end there was loud applause and many people came up to congratulate Švenk on his success.

– Prima donna Beck (*Hanuš Beck*)

One of the favorites among the boys in "Number One" was the Terezín child actor, Hanuš Beck. **Zdeněk:** He cut a fantastic figure. He was a born comedian. He had the most unlikely acquaintances; for instance I remember that Jakub Edelstein, the chairman of the Terezín "Council of Elders," lent him a bike. Karel Švenk discovered him and from then on Hanuš appeared in his cabarets. He was the child star of Terezín. He could stand alone in front of the curtain for ten minutes and amuse the audience. He had something that might best be described as an appealing cheekiness.

Hanuš Beck was the acknowledged and admired comic of Shkid. But he did not contribute to the magazine, probably because of too many other interests. And so the only things of his preserved in *Vedem* are two small articles: the preceding one, "Long Live Life" and …

Poster for the cabaret *Everything is Possible* by **Karel Švenk** (1917–1944). Jewish Museum, Prague, Neg. No. 250094. The original is in the Memorial of Terezín (the Heřman Collection).

VEDEM, Terezín 1943

Impressions
of a Poor Patient
in the Sick Bay

After a serious illness I was transferred, along with E.P., to the sick bay, from where I would like to write a short interview.

Before a chap is taken to the sick bay he has to catch a serious disease–bronchitis, for instance. Then they take him to the infirmary where they torture him for half an hour, checking to make sure his eyes are not crossed, his stomach reflexes are in order, etc. Then, because it was me, they gave me an injection. That was about four o'clock in the afternoon. We read till evening. At about midnight suddenly my neighbor Holzer calls out of his sleep: "I've got it!" and starts singing: "Ma ouz tsur jeshuaty* ... etc." Then, about four o'clock, he started singing again: "Rožnovské hodiny..." Then he stopped singing. I thought the boys were going to kill him. My friend E.P. practiced breathing all morning to see whether he still had bronchitis.

If I stay here any longer, I'll write you a letter.

(*Hanuš Beck*)

Hanuš Beck was born on September 12, 1929. He lived in Prague with his mother and sister. His sister escaped the concentration camp because at the time when the family was summoned to the transport, she was living with a family who did not fall under the Nuremberg race laws. Hanuš was deported to Terezín on April 28, 1942, and lived in Home "Number One" up to the liquidation of L 417. On September 28, 1944, he was taken to Auschwitz. They say that even on the journey there he was full of fun, and was not scared when it began to be known among the prisoners in the truck that they were not traveling to work in the "Reich" but to Auschwitz. He is supposed to have said: "Nothing will happen to me, my mother's there."

Hanuš's mother, Juliana Becková, had been arrested in the ghetto and brought to the Small Fortress by the Gestapo. From there she was deported to Auschwitz. When a transport from Terezín was expected, Mrs. Becková got in touch with the prisoners looking after the transport, who promised to do everything in their power to save her son. During the selection process Hanuš was included among those destined for work in the "Reich." But he suddenly ran over to "the other side," perhaps having seen some of his Terezín friends there. And so before the eyes of his mother's friends, Hanuš left for the gas chambers.

VEDEM, Terezín 1942–1944

Come and Act
in a Play
with Us

And act they did. They rehearsed in subzero temperatures in the attic where the wind whistled through every chink. They rehearsed assiduously, for long hours.

And it worked.

On the 14th of this month a cabaret for young people was presented on stage Q 319. Three hundred tickets were issued, though an audience three times as big could have been found.

The actors gave their best and the audience rewarded them with grateful applause. We admired the comedy duo Beck-Roth, but we must also mention the others: Lax, Marody, Grünbaum, Kauders, the lighting of Goldstein, and Löwy who was in charge of the curtain.

The experiment will be repeated in about a week, and that will give a chance to those who did not get tickets this time to see it.

– yer (*Unknown author*)

Cultural Report

The cultural program of the last fortnight has finally reached the level we were all longing for. It was as follows:

A Wolker evening was held on Sunday, January 3, in commemoration of the poet's death. We read and discussed some selected lyrics that were new to us and then Prófa dramatically recited a one-act play called *The Hospital*.

Monday Meša Stein delivered the first part of his successful lecture on the textile industry.

On Tuesday Dr. Zwicker in his lecture explained some basic economic terms to us.

On Wednesday "lights out" was moved forward to eight-fifteen in deference to Laub, who was seriously ill. This is why the second part of Meša's lecture was put off till Thursday.

On Friday Mrs. Klinkeová came to see us and sing some Hebrew songs and one aria from *The Bartered Bride*.

Fricek Pick came on Saturday and spoke fascinatingly about sport and about his own experiences in sport.

On Monday Šmuel Klauber lectured most interestingly about modern psychology.

Tuesday night we all read.

On Wednesday night Sisi Eisinger gave his lecture.

An important event in our cultural life is the re-establishment of two cultural circles (Latin and Russian).

– Cultural Correspondent (*Kurt Kotouč*)

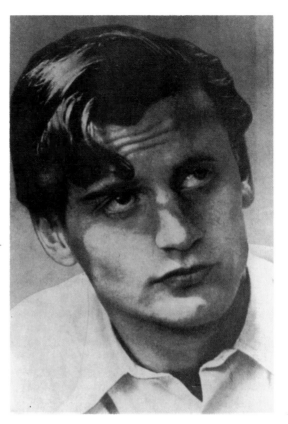

Gustav Schorsch (1918–1945). Outstanding personality in the Terezín theater performances and recitals, in which the boys from L 417 often participated. Jewish Museum, Prague, Neg. No. 24695.

everyone put on his costume. In a little while the lights came on. But what a shock! The uninitiated could have died of shock! A bear walked peacefully beside a beautiful maiden, clowns beside little old ladies, a ghetto cop next to a comedian and so on. After a while the whole conglomeration set out on a procession through the house, making the most fearful uproar. Curious spectators looked out everywhere and when the procession returned to Number One a lot of inquisitive people pushed in as well. The orchestra played a fanfare and Tiny and his comedians appeared on the stage. They all reaped a lot of applause, especially Miss Esmeralda. Laubini, Roth, Little Bull, Petr Dlouhý and many others appeared in the other sketches, and were also received with great applause (Not true!). A coffin was placed between the first and the second floor, with a guard of honor consisting of four *Leichenträger*,** the ghetto cop Hoplíček, the legionnaire Metzl, and four candle bearers, the cooks. After the funeral address by Father Bull, the funeral procession set out accompanied by the wailing of the bereaved. The procession ended at the lavatory, where the dearly departed, in accordance with his last wishes, was buried and whence, with joyful shouts, the New Year emerged in his nightshirt. With a great deal of noise, all the boys ran back to their homes.

This ends our report for the day. We wish all our listeners a good night!

– Cu – ka (*Jiří Bruml – Beno Kaufmann*)

Hello, Hello,
This is
Radio Terezín…

We are now broadcasting an account by our reporter V.:

I entered the school of L 417 and walked in the direction of Home Number One. I opened the door and saw before me a room beautifully decorated with paper chains.

I was introduced to the head of the Home, Professor E. The boys then took me straight to a corner where on a table there were five cakes, lots of sandwiches and many other things.*

Eight o'clock approached. The boys sat down at the table and in a short while the food was distributed. Between courses the boys sang "Why should we not joyful be" and other songs, mainly from *The Bartered Bride*. The lights were turned out after the meal and

* The goodies had been
  prepared from bread,
  margarine and sugar
  saved from parcels, etc.
** Corpse bearers.

The New Cultural Program of Our Home

At the beginning of this week, a great change took place in the cultural program of our Home. This is due to the extension of the regular school program, which is now taking up the time formerly devoted to the learning circles. Professor Glutty has therefore decided as follows: all existing circles are to be canceled and replaced every evening by a lecture (on literature, natural science, etc.). Furthermore there will be amusing evening programs given by our comedian, H. Beck. Two evenings will be given over to deathly silence when everybody will read or study. After these evenings we shall read to each other in bed from various entertaining or instructive books. The evening lectures will not be held, as before, only for interested parties, but for the entire Home. And finally: tomorrow, Saturday, Mařenka and Vašíček from *The Bartered Bride* will visit us. I think that everyone will have a good time.

This is all I wish to say for now. Much success to our new program.

(*Kurt Kotouč*)

Cultural Report

Last week a splendid lecture program began. So far the following lectures have been delivered: Liebstein on television, Ginz on Buddhism, Beno Kaufmann on Hinduism. We must say that these lectures are an excellent supplement to our magazine. A magazine alone is not enough for cultural life, because articles exceeding the usual format cannot be accepted, regardless of how valuable they may be. The value of the lectures is confirmed not only by the interest shown by the listeners, but also by the increasing number of lecturers, who are preparing some excellent talks for us: Mühlstein on Mozart, Kahn on old Czech, Weil on the history of chess, Roth on Cervantes, Kotouč on criminality. But there is one thing we miss – lectures by adults. For not one of us has sufficient knowledge to talk about political trends and ideologies. I hope that this gap will soon be filled.

– nz (*Petr Ginz*)

Eva Wollsteinerová
(b. 1931, perished).
"Table with Christmas Tree."
Crayons, pencil,
280 × 210 mm.
Jewish Museum, Prague,
Inv. No. 131733.

Emil Utitz
(1883–1956).
Jewish Museum, Prague,
Neg. No. 24826.

Poster for the Terezín
lectures of Professor **Emil
Utitz**.
Jewish Museum, Prague,
Neg. No. 24911. The
original is in the Memorial
of Terezín (the Heřman
Collection).

VORTRÄGE
Universitäts-Prof. Dr. Emil Utitz
Themen:

* Its first official name was
the *Zentral-
ghettobücherei*,
established at the end of
1942. From 1944 on it
was called the
"Community Library."
The Nazis permitted it so
they could demonstrate
the "civilized" face of
Terezín. Smaller libraries
were also established –
medical, technical and the
youth library mentioned
in this article. The
Ghettobücherei, which by
liberation contained about
130,000 volumes, was
supervised with great
dedication by the
outstanding Prague
philosopher and
aesthetician Professor
Emil Utitz.

The Young People's Library in L 216

I should like to give you a short report of the Young People's Library which opened this week in L 216. The idea of setting up such a library arose five months ago in the circle of teenagers who had previously looked after the cultural youth program. It only became possible to put this into practice a few weeks ago by amalgamating the private libraries L 216 and Q 609, the Dresden barracks library for the young, and a contribution from the *Ghettobücherei*.* This nucleus, about 2,000 volumes, was increased by books from individual members who had to hand over at least two books in return for borrowing one, or one book if they wanted to read in the reading room. Now the library contains about 35,000 volumes and interest among the youth of Terezín is constantly growing. Valuable books are only available in the reading room. Others may be taken out. The library contains Czech and German literature, boys' books, various scientific texts, and books on Judaism and Zionism.

The library also contains a permanent exhibition of visual art. Every evening there is a program at the library, either a musical evening, a lecture or a slide show.

It has never happened before in Terezín, that by combining something private, something public has been created.

(*Herbert Maier*)

The Magic Flute

The Magic Flute is the last opera composed by the famous composer W. A. Mozart, written in the year of his death. Emanuel Schikaneder, who wrote the libretto, and Mozart himself were both Freemasons. This is why the libretto so clearly shows the Freemasons' thoughts and tendencies, and the whole opera is regarded not as a German national opera, as some have said, but as the opera of the Freemasons. At that time Austria was against the Freemasons and because of censorship, the libretto became incomprehensible and, as is the case with most operas, worthless and nonsensical.

The opera contains separate arias connected by dialogue. The action is as follows: "The fainting prince Tamino is attacked by a huge snake and rescued by three court ladies of the Queen of the Night. When he regains consciousness she shows him a picture of her daughter. He immediately falls in love with her and the Queen asks him to free her from the clutches of the High Priest Sarastro who has abducted her. Tamino, led by three small boys, sets out at once to rescue Pamina. When he reaches Sarastro, the priest convinces him that the Queen is evil and that he is holding Pamina for her own well-being and liberty. Tamino becomes a good, free man and both are happy."

There are many remarkable scenes in this opera. *The Magic Flute* is one of Mozart's most beautiful operas, where his light style, so difficult for the singers, is put to best use. There is not an opera house that does not have this wonderful work in its repertoire, and this is why we in Terezín do not wish to lag behind. Raf Schächter, with his excellent cast, has rehearsed *The Magic Flute*, and we shall soon be able to hear it.

– Pinťa (*Emanuel Mühlstein*)*

Vlasta Schönová recites *May* by Mácha in L 203 on May 18 at 6:30 p.m.

The attic of the house L 203, twilight, a stuffy atmosphere, the stink of sweat, fifty to seventy persons crowding into several square meters of space. Gong … we did not take in the words of Mácha's *May* because of the music of this performance, the hymn to woods, warm rains in the night, the song of the wind in the crowns of century-old trees. There is no need for words, and as much is said by Smetana's *Vltava* or Liszt's *Hungarian Rhapsody*.

Vlasta Schönová's recitation was perfect. She caught the soul of the part, lived it. It was a song and an image. Her expression, her movements, the picturesque aspect of the part, are the expression of an inner culture. This was the synthesis of interior and exterior of the role she delineated.

The beauty of the spoken word, this recitation of Mácha's *May*, is in effect a translation into all the languages of the world, an international symphony of *the living word*. A Jewish actress, assimilated artistically into the Czech, has paid her debt to world culture.

– Pepek (*Josef Stiassny*)

* He played the part of Pepíček in the children's opera *Brundibár*.

Entrance ticket for Terezín cultural programs. Jewish Museum, Prague, Neg. No. 29097.

Poster for the Terezín lectures of **Nora Fried** (Norbert Frýd, 1913–1976). Jewish Museum, Prague, Neg. No. 24912. The original is in the Memorial of Terezín (the Heřman Collection).

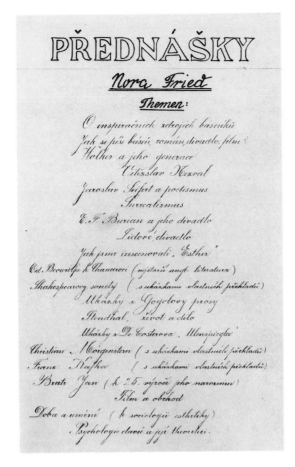

Terezín Cultural Program of the Week:
Theater: Petr Kien, *Puppets*
Švenk, Karel, *Long Live Life*
Schönová, *May*

Tickets and Information
Cultural Correspondent
(*Kurt Kotouč*)

Reportage About *Esther*

All of you are sure to remember that some time ago Nora Frýd came to see us. He told us also about old Czech folk plays and as an illustration he brought us a comedy entitled *Esther*. We all examined it with interest and were amazed at the strange style and the uneven verses of the Czech peasant who was its author. The play itself dates from about the seventeenth century, the time of rococo and baroque. The plot is essentially the same as the bible story. And in many places the play is enlivened by dance, song, and straight scenes, like the appearance of the peasants, the cook, the butler, etc. The play has two parts. There is never a dull moment. Some-thing is happening all the time to keep the audience's attention. The staging is note-worthy. The stage is divided by curtains into three sections. Center stage is permanently allotted to the king, the left to the queen, the right to Haman and less important charac-ters like Mordechai, the courtiers, the exe-cutioner, etc. The proscenium is used by all three of them. This clever and simple idea came from the director E. F. Burian, who in-tended to rehearse and perform *Esther* in Prague but was forbidden to do so by the "au-thorities" because of its "pro-Jew" stance. Although the different actions sometimes take place several kilometers apart, in the king's palace and in town, for instance, the division of the stage makes it possible to make transitions smoothly. We can observe these scenes side by side, without ruining the effect. Music for *Esther* was composed by Karel Reiner, who worked in close collaboration with E. F. Burian, as did the director Nora Frýd. The songs, with the exception of a few merry dance songs, are written in the manner of old Czech church chorales (like Mordechai's prayer to God). The songs will be accompanied by an orchestra of five mu-sicians: violin, bass, trumpet, clarinet and drum.

It might be of interest to quote from the play. The first peasant asks about the king's scepter: "That staff is nothing but a twisted stick," and the other answers with true peas-ant forthrightness: "Come on, good fellow, don't be such a hick!" Or Mordechai's speech before King Ahasver, when he sup-ports his testimony with the words: "… and I can swear to that on my death!" There are a hundred and more such humorous scenes in *Esther*.

Let us hope that *Esther* will not end up like all the plays that we have so far rehearsed, and that we'll soon be hearing excellent re-views of our performance directly from the theatrical experts of Terezín.

– Fi–La (A company with a very limited liabil-ity; *probably Herbert Fischl – Petr Lax*)

The Prague composer Hans Krása lived in the camp. Choirmaster Ruda Franěk rehearsed his opera *Brundibár* with the children, which, given the number of repeat performances, overshadowed everything else, including the success of *The Bartered Bride*.

(Norbert Frýd: Letters in a Bottle)

Brundibár

Hans Krása: *Brundibár*. Two scenes from the Nazi propaganda film "The Führer Has Given Them a Town," shot in Terezín in 1944. For the purpose of filming, the performance of the children's opera had to be transferred from the Magdeburg barracks to the large hall of the Terezín Sokol gymnasium, which until then had been out of bounds to the prisoners. **František Zelenka** had to design new sets for the much larger stage. Jewish Museum, Prague, Neg. Nos. 20052, 24750.

Brundibár the Organ Grinder – the children's opera that enjoyed an endless number of repeat performances in front of Terezín audiences – was a well-deserved success. I have no wish to quarrel with the quality of the libretto or the music, or speculate on whether it was properly directed. That is a matter for the critics and for the people who watched it from the auditorium. But I can say that the effort put into the children's opera was far from small and it was not easy, in the comparatively short time of one-and-a-half months, to rehearse a ten-man orchestra, a forty-member children's choir, and ten soloists, who were also children. Or have you ever been a director who has had to deal with fifty strapping boys and girls who are convinced that the more noise and fun during the rehearsals the better? No – it's not easy and I take my hat off to Rudi Freudenfeld, because throughout the rehearsals he only got angry a few times, and then calmed down again immediately. I would not have had that kind of patience, and I doubt whether anybody else would have either.

To give you the story of *Brundibár* from its origin to the first night: the first rehearsals

were mostly boring. They were held in a dusty attic with a screeching harmonium and suffocating heat. The choir sang "This is little Pepíček ..." twice, learned another verse, repeated "Brundibár defeated ..." and then gladly escaped the stifling atmosphere to get a breath of fresh air. In the meantime the candidates for solo parts stood with trembling voices before the sweating Rudi and sang "Lalalalala" after him. We were on tenterhooks to know who would get what part and who would say a few more words than anyone else on the stage. There was plenty of competition, envy, and minor intrigue, but at last all the roles were assigned and slowly but surely we started to rehearse. At first, we only rehearsed the songs.

The rehearsals were soporific, though some people enjoyed them, and it often seemed the whole business would come to a bad end. But some sort of aura held us to-

gether, the feeling that "when it's finished, it'll be super." We made progress, we got a better rehearsal room, and interest grew. Everybody began to look forward to rehearsals, and would tell his acquaintances with a certain pride, "We're rehearsing a children's opera."

At last the day came when we could sing nearly the whole opera. Architect Zelenka came and we started to set up the staging. Perhaps it was because we suddenly had to get off our seats and move about as if we had a stage, or perhaps it was architect Zelenka with his: "What are you staring at, you fool," or "Get a move on, don't stand about like a lot of drunks." The fact is that everything suddenly came to life, and the rehearsals became so exiting that Rudi finally threatened to drop everything if things went on like this, that we'd never amount to anything, etc. Fortunately nobody took him seriously, and so "mix-up after mix-up" continued to be the order of the day in most rehearsals. The director's job was not easy, for what can you do with a fellow who insists on singing "Who's afraid of the actor ..." instead of "the doctor," or with an individual who always jumps in a bar ahead. There were quite a number of people like that and it took some time to get rid of them. Unfortunately the spirit of these types still haunts the performances, causing all sorts of foul-ups. By that time, the newly appointed conductor, Rudi Freudenfeld, was already rehearsing with the orchestra. The work was beginning to come together, and only small adjustments had to be made. The last week of rehearsals

Hans Krása
(1899–1944),
composer.
Jewish Museum, Prague,
Neg. No. 24951.

155

came (we were now in the Magdeburg barracks) and there was no shortage of mishaps. The least upsetting was that during one of the final rehearsals the lights in the Magdeburg barracks went out at half past nine. What happened before this whistling, screaming, shouting throng of rehearsing actors was called to order defies description. Suffice it to say we left a partly destroyed stage behind and were in giddy mood.

Then came the dress rehearsal, which was actually a disappointment to everyone. We all expected noise, confusion, disorder, all of which is the sign of real theater life, and hoped that it would be full of mishaps, which could be taken as a sure sign that the opening night would go well. But as I said before, we were all properly disappointed. It must have been the most peaceful dress rehearsal ever held in Terezín, and a most successful one.

Despite that, the premiere came off splendidly. We arrived an hour and a half before curtain, and when we saw each other in our makeup, which we thought terrible, we began to cut up as usual, till Rudi had to come and settle us down. But as soon as the audience started filing in, our little souls were slowly but surely overcome by stage fright. Three of the "experienced" actors walked up and down backstage and said over and over again: "I haven't got stage fright, nothing can throw me off," and only their scarlet ears belied them. But as soon as the first bars of music sounded, we forgot our fear and went to it. Everything went well. Brundibár – Sára Trechlinger – on stage with the artisans, saw to it that there was a lot of fun, while Pepíček, Anička and the animals took care of the musical side of things. And the lullaby sung by the choir, "Mummy is rocking ..." moved everyone and reaped well-deserved applause. Rafík Schächter, after all, had worked like a galley slave to get us to sing it

properly. And when we had finished and the hall was filled with thunderous applause, we were all happy and content, for man is a creature eager for fame. And in all of us there was some satisfaction at having done a thing well.

Now, in further performances, we've all got the singing down to a routine and can concentrate on making sure there's a lot of fun. There have been unforseen occurrences, though. One performance was suddenly interrupted by a terrified scream from twenty maidenly throats. After anxious enquiries, we discovered that a bench holding twenty singers had tumbled over. But often things happen on stage that the audience doesn't even notice, while we backstage are doubled over with laughter.

Brundibár will soon disappear from the thoughts of those who watched it in Terezín, but for us actors it will remain one of the few beautiful memories we have of that place.

– ini (*Rudolf Lauf*)

About the Children's Opera

One fine day Mr. XY asked his promising son: "How did you enjoy the theater?"

His son answers brightly, "You know, Daddy, it was all right, but the music sounded a bit like a siren."

Father: "Was it happy or funny?"

"Well, you know, the meaning was serious, but it was very funny."

"Oh, I see. Well, I suppose I had better go and see for myself."

(*Unknown author*)

Cultural Report

Two lectures were given last week: Hanuš Weil on The History of Chess and Pepek Taussig and Nora Frýd on Gogol. The first lecture was extremely well prepared and little Weil delivered it faultlessly from memory. But I'm afraid it wasn't very original. It is not the task of the lecturer to spew out the text of a book he used for research, but to gather material and, like a bee turning nectar into honey, suck out the most relevant material from his reading, digest it, and deliver a lecture in his own words.

The second lecture was one of the best ever given in the Home. But I must still take Pepek Taussig to task over something. I am sure you noticed that whenever he got stuck he reached for a joke as though it were a life preserver. Mass-produced jokes and anecdotes are like ready-wrapped presents with the inscription: "Wishing you all the very best ..." Whenever he was hard up, Pepek managed to shake one out of his sleeve.

Pepek's lecture was most instructive, and told us a lot not only about Gogol, but also about the era that contributed to his formation. I would criticize Nora for overacting while reading his excerpts, and a little less gesticulation would not have hurt either. But the conclusion of his lecture was impressive and fiery... On the whole it was successful.

We are greatly looking forward to the lecture cycle on Russian writers.

– nz (*Petr Ginz*)

The Picture

You painters of Terezín,
Letting a little bluish water
Float in a small jasper dish,
You creatures – be human.
You who mix the yellow of hunch-backed barracks
Silently and smoothly
With the bright red of the roofs
On sunny days,

This is not a flamboyant event
You are painting.
These are only small clouds, and dreaming,
And cursed dead walls.

This is not the world. They are only walls,
A carnival of colors, a world of sun and precious stones.
It is the great sun, light in the universe
And bitter beauty, bitter, terrifying illusions.

You painters of Terezín, who let wide windows
Open to the world, float against
A backdrop of clouds in your silent idylls:
One day you will tumble into mouths open in agony.
Get rid of ellipses that lead to the abyss,
And live, create in darkness!

– Ha- (*Hanuš Hachenburg*)

Margit Gerstmannová
(b. 1931, perished).
"Terezín motif."
Collage, 320 × 210 mm.
Jewish Museum, Prague,
Inv. No. 121760.

Negroes and Us

Not long ago I read *Uncle Tom's Cabin* by Harriet Beecher Stowe. You all surely know the book. It tells the life story of several black slaves in America. Many of the horrors of negro slavery are described in the book, the beatings, the starvation, and so on. But most of all I was moved by the splitting up of families. Many slave families were waiting in the slave markets to be auctioned off. Their only wish was to be sold together to one master. But not even this smallest desire was granted. They were each sold separately, and would probably never meet again. This is how negro slaves were sold and treated in America in the nineteenth century, that is to say, three hundred years after the discovery of America.

How do we differ from those slaves, and how do our times differ from those times? We live here in Terezín, in a slave warehouse. Just like the negroes, we are subjected to beatings and hunger. The one way in which we perhaps differ is the irregular and unjustified splitting up of families. But even this

159

is now happening. On January 29, 1944, young men and old, sons, fathers, brothers, relatives were sent away by transport. This is happening to us Jews, a persecuted people. Just like the negroes, Tom and the three others, we bear our fate calmly and heroically, looking it straight in the eye. On April 2, 1944, when they actually boarded the train that was to take them away into the far unknown, I stood on the street corner with the crowd to see many friends, perhaps for the last time, while others took leave of their relatives. Then the slave owner* dressed in a green uniform and cap, called the overseer,** telling him to allow those dogs onto the train to say farewell to the departing. Not long afterward, the train left, and word soon spread like wildfire through Terezín about the decency and compassion of the slave owner who had allowed his slaves to say farewell to their children, their fathers, their brothers, their loved ones.

So how do we really differ from those ignorant black slaves, now, at a time of great cultural flowering, in the middle of the twentieth century? Could not a book called *Mr. Kohn's Garret*** be written to stand beside *Uncle Tom's Cabin*?

(*Hanuš Pollak*)

* This probably refers to SS commandant Rahm.
** Probably the commandant of gendarmes, Janáček.
*** By partitioning the extensive lofts in the buildings and barracks of Terezín, "garrets" or "cubby holes" were created to serve as private and very often illegal lodgings. But only a very few of the prisoners could afford this "luxury."
**** Rosh Hashanah, the New Year holiday, is the beginning of the Hebrew month called Tishrey, which falls in September or October. The Hebrew calendar is based on the lunar cycle synchronized with the solar year. Each Hebrew month begins with the appearance of a new moon.

Preparing for the High Holiday

I noticed an interesting psychological feature in myself this week: How even an unbeliever and atheist can be drawn against his will into the emotions surrounding the high holidays. *Rosh Hashanah**** is the first link in a chain of ten days, when every Jew searches his soul, scrutinizes his actions over the last year, weighs them on the scales of his impersonalized sense of justice and, before his conscience or before his god, confesses all his sins, repents and promises to make amends.

Not even I could escape the atmosphere enveloping Terezín in the days of *Rosh Hashanah*, an atmosphere whose special aroma was so sweetly familiar to me from the days of my orthodox past. But in my case, it indicated a special kind of contemplation. I did not examine so much my own past actions, but rather those of the people around me. Not that I regard myself as infallible and free from sin, but I said to myself that my own actions – the sinful ones in particular – are only a tiny drop in the affairs of the world, and perhaps most of them could be explained by the evil influence of what is going on around, which makes them, both from the human point of view and from that of God's justice (if such a thing exists), pardonable. It is of no great interest to me, in any case. I am not praying for a long life, or an easy death, or forgiveness for all my sins. I am more interested in knowing what attitude I should take to the sins of the world around me. The world is swimming in a sea of war crimes. Its depths are unmeasurable. So I ask myself: how should I behave towards the perpetrators of that war? Is the German nation as a whole guilty? Should our hatred, our just rage, and our judgment come down on them all, without distinction? As a people who have undergone such immense suffering as a result of this war, who have been demoted to a status below that of the creature called man, we are particularly prone to hating them all indiscriminately. The secret wish of most of us is that a certain part of the European continent should be blown to smithereens, with not a stone left standing. We allow ourselves to be carried away by our feelings, and do not think rationally.

But it is more important now than ever before that the good Lord should preserve us with our reason intact. Do we want to reciprocate with the same unjust hatred that we are suffering under at the moment? It is not my intention to deliver a philanthropic address like the Salvation Army, nor am I a missionary for the old Christian morality – forgive those that have sinned against us. I am fully aware of Wolker's words: We must hate some of the people in order that we might love most of the people.

I do not want to give you ready answers. That would be too easy. Nor do I wish to say straight out: Let us love these and hate those. I shall try to outline a method that is less easy, one that will force you to think and draw your own conclusions.

By a most unusual chance I discovered, on the eve of *Rosh Hashanah*, a notebook of mine that I had considered long lost, a notebook containing my notes on Eckermann's conversations with Goethe. It was these dialogues that inspired me to write this article. Let me quote some of Goethe's sayings, that they might become the basis for our thoughts and our conclusions!

"He who would act justly, need never condemn, need never consider what perversity is, but must only act well. It is not a question of tearing down, but of building up, what could become a source of joy to humanity."

"Much can be achieved through strictness, more through love, most however through acknowledgment and impartial justice, where no consideration is given to the personal."

"I often think of my novel *Wilhelm Meister*, where the idea is expressed that all people make up the sum total of mankind, and that we are worthy of respect only insofar as we respect mankind as a whole."

"I like observing foreign peoples, and I would advise everyone to do the same. National literature today has nothing to say. The epoch of world literature has begun and everyone must try to advance it."

"The poet loves his country as a man and a citizen, but the land of his poetic power and his poetic acts is goodness, nobility and beauty, which are bound to no particular region and to no particular country. In this he is like the eagle who, with vision free, soars above all countries. Then what do love of one's country and patriotism mean? They mean fighting against all harmful prejudices, eliminating narrow-minded views, enlightening the spirit of one's own nation, purifying its taste and ennobling its thoughts and sentiments. Can anyone do better than that? Does acting patriotically mean anything else? "

"The only important thing is how one weighs in on the scales of humanity. Everything else is conceit."

"I never behaved with affectation in my poetry. I never wrote about, nor gave expression to, something I had never experienced or what did not burn my fingers. I only sang songs of love when I loved. How could I sing songs of hate without ever having felt hatred? And just between ourselves, I never hated the French, although I thanked the Lord when we got rid of them. How could I, to whom the only matters of principal importance are culture and barbarity, hate a nation that is one of the most cultured in the world, and to whom, to a great extent, I owe my education? … National hatred is altogether a strange thing. It is at its most powerful and most vehement on the lowest levels of culture. But there is a level where it completely disappears and where to some extent we stand above nations, and feel the fortunes or misfortunes of neighboring nations as if they were our own. This cultural level is consistent with my nature."

– Tiny (*Valtr Eisinger*)

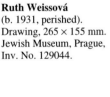

Ruth Weissová
(b. 1931, perished).
Drawing, 265 × 155 mm.
Jewish Museum, Prague,
Inv. No. 129044.

Recollections
of Mrs. Věra Sommerová,
Valtr Eisinger's Wife

In the summer of 1940 the German fascists issued a decree according to which Jewish children were forbidden to attend any type of Protectorate school. I was due to enter the eighth (highest) form and at the end of it sit for my university entrance exam. After a long search we learned that it was possible to finish grammar school in only one institute in the entire Protectorate, which happened to be in Brno. It was a Reform grammar school.

For the first term I was an external student, but that was very difficult because I didn't have the necessary textbooks. For the second term – with the permission from the Protectorate authorities – I left for Brno to finish school and take my entrance exam. It was when taking my end-of-term exams as an external student that I first met my Czech teacher, Professor Valtr Eisinger.

To this day I remember the subject I got for composition: "An apple tree in bloom." Czech was my favorite subject, and so I tried to give rein to my fantasy on this poetic topic.

Even then my teacher made a strong impression on me. He was a young, good-looking, pleasant man, very friendly and informal. He had come to the Jewish grammar school in Brno for the same reasons as the rest of us: he was not allowed to teach anywhere else.

The closer spring came, the more intensely I felt that the lessons in Czech literature were the most interesting of all my subjects – and the more our "eye contact" increased, as Valtr would insist later on. We felt that something had to happen. One fine March day the school superintendent (also a man excluded by the regime) brought me a letter and, at the same time, requested that I not mention its contents to my fellow pupils. With my heart pounding in my throat I read the first lines of the letter: "I do not want to address you as social conventions require, I cannot address you as I would like, therefore forgive me if this letter has no salutation at all."

This is how the romantic, secret love of a twenty-eight-year-old teacher for his nineteen-year-old pupil began, and it survived the most cruel tests life could offer.

In Brno we met every day from March 24 on until I was forced to leave after the premature closing of the school by the Germans in May, 1941. We always met at the terminus of some tram line. Řečkovice, Baba, and the other outskirts of Brno were the most beautiful spots on the planet that spring. By then we were no longer allowed to leave our lodgings after eight o'clock, and so I had the whole evenings free to study. And although times were bad and we had no idea what would become of us, we planned a future together. Valtr never doubted the outcome of the Nazi military adventure. During our walks we discussed what would happen after the war and what the world would be like.

After I returned home (we had moved to

Solopysky near Horní Černošice after our house in Kralupy was confiscated) Valtr and I wrote to each other at least twice a week. Not just I, but my entire family waited impatiently for his letters. Although my parents did not know Valtr personally, they grew very fond of him through his letters and through what I had told them. He was always direct, honorable and sincere, and my mother declared she loved him like her own son.

Then terrible news came: in January, 1942, Valtr was sent to the concentration camp of Terezín and our correspondence was reduced to the occasional postcard with no more than thirty printed words on it. But even then, in those meager lines, he was able to express what he felt and let me know he was constantly thinking of me.

In September, 1942, we met again in Terezín, where my whole family had been deported. Even though conditions there were very bad – with hunger, disease, a lack of the basic hygienic necessities, the overcrowded little town, the exhausting work, the constant fear of transports into the unknown – I was able to bear it all easily in Valtr's presence, and as a matter of fact, it was the happiest time of my life, because I was certain of his love, his devotion and I knew that I could always rely on him.

We both worked in Youth Care. Valtr was the leader of a Youth Home for boys, and he often spoke of them to me. He tried to be not just a pedagogue, but a friend, a counselor, and a confidential adviser. I started to work as a nurse in a children's home and later moved to a kindergarten. I had no experience at all with children, but I was very fond of them, and felt terribly sorry for them and the conditions in which they had to live. The children felt that. Whenever we appeared with Valtr in the streets of Terezín our children would come flocking to us. We used to joke about how our work never seemed to end. We had long discussions about the individual children and how best to handle them. The children all had strong personalities, both the little ones, from four to six years old, and Valtr's thirteen- and fourteen-year-old boys.

In Terezín, as his fiancée, my name was added to Valtr's identity card and the SS men promised that they would not forcibly separate us and that if one went into a transport, the other would be able to go along. My parents, with my siblings, had to leave in December, 1943, for Birkenau (the name of the camp in Auschwitz) and I was left in Terezín with Valtr and his mother. Valtr's father was seriously ill and died shortly after the departure of this transport. Valtr looked after me with great care and tried to ease my sorrow at the departure of my family as best he could. I could scarcely abide the thought that all my family had gone into the unknown, that I was no longer with them, and that I might never see them again.

I had always dreamt of getting married after the war in normal circumstances, surrounded by our families. But then came June, 1944, with the threat of new transports. We were still afraid they wouldn't let us leave together and so we asked for permission for a Terezín wedding, which would entitle us to be regarded as husband and wife, would protect us from forced separation, and enabled the woman to add the name of her husband to her maiden name.

On June 11 we were married at the Terezín town hall. We kept our wedding a secret to the last minute, but imagine our surprise when the children found out and prepared us a celebration we would never have dreamt of under normal circumstances. At half past ten the Terezín town hall was overflowing with children, their parents and our colleagues, the child care workers. Overnight, my colleagues from the kindergarten had taught the poor little ones a congratulatory rhyme. First a group of Czech children, then a German group (deported from Germany) recited. Finally the child-care workers formed a canopy over our heads with their hands, and we marched out of the town hall. Every child handed us a marguerite. I had a whole armful. These flowers, and a wedding bouquet of irises, had been smuggled into the ghetto by a group of agricultural workers – prisoners who worked outside the gates of Terezín. There were no flowers in Terezín. In front of the town hall Valtr's boys silently formed a double line behind us and with great ceremony walked with us to the Home, where they had prepared a fantastic present – a huge cake made from buns they had saved from their weekly rations. Poor boys, all of us looked forward every week to this one brick-hard delicacy, and they had given up this pleasure for us. With the help of some wartime custard powder one of the mothers had turned them into a cake. Valtr received a lovely fountain pen from his boys as a wedding present. I wanted the cake to be divided up at once among everyone at the Home

Karel Berman
(b. 1919, survived). Jewish Museum, Prague, Neg. No. 30032.

Poster for Verdi's *Requiem* rehearsed under Rafael Schächter by the prisoners in 1943–1944. Accompanied on the piano by composer Gideon Klein, an outstanding personality of musical life in the ghetto. Among the soloists was Karel Berman, who survived the concentration camp and later became one of the outstanding soloists of the National Theatre, Prague, and a professor at the Academy of Music, also in Prague. Jewish Museum, Prague, Neg. No. 25088. The original is in the Memorial of Terezín (the Heřman Collection).

and eaten on the spot, but the boys wouldn't hear of it. It was their contribution, they said, to our wedding feast. And it was a grand feast indeed – herbal tea sweetened with saccharine and other goodies made from the same hard buns.

In the afternoon we invited a group of former schoolmates and teachers from the Brno grammar school to the garret that had been built within the school premises by the minders themselves. In the evening we invited another group of colleagues from Youth Care that also lived in the school. In between Valtr rushed off to sing Verdi's *Requiem* with the choir conducted by Rafael Schächter. Valtr had a nice tenor voice, and he enjoyed singing. He even sang the solo part of the Principal in *The Bartered Bride*, and singing under Schächter gave him a tremendous psychological lift in that atmosphere full of stress and worry. There were few tenors in the choir at that time. Transports were leaving all the time, and the trained choir was badly depleted. So we agreed that on our wedding day, Valtr would go to strengthen the tenor section. I got a free ticket, for which there was always a great demand.

Rafík Schächter was tremendous. When the concert ended, to huge applause, he congratulated us on our marriage in front of the entire audience and ended up by embracing and kissing us. How often I would remember our wedding *Requiem*, which perhaps was the portent of tragic events to come.

Even after the wedding, we lived separately, as did practically all the other married couples in Terezín. It was only after the liquidation of the school, which was taken over by the Nazis,

and after moving into the former fire hall that we managed to get a small space for ourselves, a separate corner in the large hall (2×2m), exactly one bunk length square. That was the pinnacle of happiness for us. How glad I was to have this miniature household. We fitted the tiny corner up with love and care. It was most primitive, but we thought it the height of luxury.

After a fortnight of the happiest days we had ever known, a further catastrophe struck. The Nazis ordered transports made up entirely of men, and Valtr was included in one of the first. I did not behave heroically at all. I was a complete wreck, I cried wherever I went – life lost its meaning for me. When I realized that my Valtr, this impractical, absent-minded professor, honest to a fault and as clumsy with his hands as they came, would be exposed to further torture and hardship amidst hunger and filth, and that I should not be with him, that we should constantly be worried and afraid for each other – that was unimaginable to me.

By chance I learned that only 500 men would be included in the fifth transport and the rest, up to a thousand, would be made up of women who volunteered to go with their husbands. It was another favorite trick of the Nazis, who so often before had not kept their promises. I rushed around Terezín looking for someone to arrange it for me to be together with Valtr as soon as possible. What would he say if I did not come? After all, we had promised each other that I would use every opportunity to stay with him. Finally, after many interventions, I succeeded and, overjoyed, I squeezed into the crowded train.

Instead of sending us to a labor camp in Germany, as they had promised, we found they had sent us to Auschwitz. The infamous Doctor Mengele picked us both out in the selection process, though he very nearly excluded me because I seemed too weak. I learned only later that this would have meant the gas chamber. By way of welcome, the SS man guarding us shot a girl from one of the camps we passed by. Some people had called out to us that they were hungry and asked us to throw them some food. A can was tossed over the fence from the midst of our procession and when a young girl caught it, the SS man shot at her and she fell into the dirt with blood gushing from her face. That put an end to my illusions about humane behavior.

When they locked us up in that terrible women's camp, where there was no hope of even catching sight of our men, I was so distraught and apathetic that I had only one wish: to dig a hole in the earth and disappear underground like a mole, to hear nothing, see nothing, feel nothing. Then I went apathetically and passively through all the selection processes, praying that Valtr would not see me in this miserable state, in rags, filthy, and with my head shaved.

I learned about Valtr through the mother of one of the boys from Valtr's home, who worked in the Auschwitz prisoners' self-administration. She said he was in the men's camp and that he was trying to catch a glimpse of me at least through the wires when going to work. Before this was possible, we were sent to Germany with a women's transport, to the labor camp in Freiberg, Saxony, and I never saw my Valtr again. He later went to Buchenwald and is said to have been shot on January 15, 1945, during the March of Death.

All I have left are memories and a handful of letters kept in a hiding place during the war. They are memories of a man whose place in my life was never filled by anybody else. Even after thirty years, those letters are still full of the deep love and tenderness he was capable of giving to his nearest and dearest.

VEDEM, Terezín 1943

Rambles Through Terezín: Wedding

Magdeburg barracks, Number 118, the auditorium of the Terezín theater. Eleven o'clock, the sober light of an April morning, and, among the darkened lights and sets of an operating theater, about fifty young people. The atmosphere of a school graduation photograph, young men in borrowed hats and dark, borrowed clothes. The bridegroom, a youth who up to the very last minute chatters loudly with a group of comrades. The bride, a seventeen-year-old girl, who only an hour ago removed her sweatsuit and in a few hours, as Mrs. XYZ and dressed in work clothes, will transport cases, mattresses, or planks through the streets of Terezín on a funeral cart.

Two silver candles, a cup with "wine" in it, black coffee, three rabbis, a canopy. The first rabbi is looking for matches and can't find any, nor can the second or the third. The men check their pockets. No one has matches. Finally the young mother-in-law, the bridegroom's mother, fishes some matches out of her pocket with the sure, swift movement of a chain smoker. Bride and bridegroom are standing under the canopy, the rabbi says the words of the vow in Hebrew, the bridegroom repeats after him. The second rabbi sings some psalms, the third rabbi, half in German and half in Hebrew, mumbles something about a journey together through life, commitments, marriage according to the Jewish rites. The theater, the comedy, the third-rate actors, the

set depicting an operating theater – this is the
**Terezín surrealism of everyday life. Two
burning candles in heavy candlesticks, the
young men getting ready to toss not only the
bridegroom but also (oh horror) the bride,
high into the air. The synagogue becomes
a theater once more. On stage Růžička's
group is reciting Erben.**

– Pepek (*Josef Stiassny*)

Marie: Věra, did you know Valtr Eisinger's
family?
Věra: As a matter of fact, I didn't meet
Valtr's family until we got to Terezín. But in
Brno, Valtr used to talk to me a lot about his
parents and his brothers and sisters, and later he
also wrote about them. Valtr's father was a retail
livestock trader. When he was about thirty, he
caught a cold on one of his trips and from then
on he suffered from arthritis. Eventually he
could only walk on crutches. It was Valtr's
mother who held the family together. She was
a dressmaker in Podivín. Valtr had two siblings.
His elder brother Bruno was apprenticed to
a shoemaker and his sister Marta studied at the
conservatory. Later she became a piano teacher.
I had already been in Terezín for some time
when Valtr's family arrived. Naturally I was
nervous about meeting them. I had been ill for
a long time and I was afraid I wouldn't make
a good impression. There were nine nurses sharing my room and they all helped me get ready
for the event. They put rouge on my cheeks so
I wouldn't look so pale. Then my sister came
and got terribly upset and told me to wash it off
immediately. What would Valtr's family think,
seeing me painted like that?
Marie: And how did Valtr's family welcome
you?
Věra: The first thing Valtr's mother said was,
"Good Lord, look how young she is. She's only
a child, and she's supposed to be Valtr's future
wife?" But later, when I started to take care of
Valtr, she said: "I thought you wouldn't know
how to do anything, but now you've taken over
and there's nothing of Valtr left for me, not even
his dirty laundry…"
Marie: Wasn't Valtr nervous about meeting
your family?
Věra: I know that Valtr always said his family
were great individualists, and that he was afraid
of what they might say when he brought me
home. But nervous about my family? No, certainly not. Father sometimes made fun of him
because of his ideals, but otherwise they got on
well. Valtr hit it off especially well with my
sister Vlasta. Father always said we didn't need
to marry someone of outstanding position. His
greatest fear was that his children should not
behave appropriately, that they would live
above their circumstances. It didn't matter at all
to him that Valtr had a small salary. He expected
him to support his family, that went without
saying. He used to say, never marry a layabout
or a loafer, who couldn't make his own way
even if he is from a well-off family. He re-
spected Valtr, who sent half his earnings home,
very much.
Marie: How did Valtr manage to finish his studies when his family had no resources?

Věra: I think he had a scholarship. But he always lived very modestly. From Brno he regularly sent six hundred crowns of his teacher's salary home and lived on the other six hundred. He had only one suit, always carefully cleaned and brushed …

Marie: How did you imagine your future life with Valtr?

Věra: First of all we didn't know how long the war would last. In May, 1941, the Nazis forbade us to take our university entrance exam and I went home to Solopysky. Valtr and I corresponded the whole time. And when the threat of transports started in Prague, Valtr offered to protect me, first through a marriage by proxy, which would become valid if I were included in a transport. I couldn't bring myself to do it at the time. I was still far too closely tied to my family. I couldn't imagine living somewhere else with Valtr if my parents were taken away. In the end everything turned out differently. Valtr left eight months earlier than we did. He wrote how glad he was that we hadn't married, that I hadn't had go with him, that he hoped we would meet after the war as free people.

Marie: How did Valtr receive you in Terezín?

Věra: Valtr's presence made my arrival much easier. He knew when I was coming because he checked the lists regularly, so he was waiting for us. He'd arranged to be a porter. I introduced Valtr to my parents – they only knew him from his letters – and everybody liked him. Later on, when Valtr's parents came, we arranged a great family meeting in the yard of the barracks. Everything turned out well. Valtr used to go with me to see my mother and sister. Sometimes when we got a parcel containing a soup thickener and potatoes, mother made potato soup as a supper supplement to the meager Terezín rations. And of course she invited Valtr, and it was all the talk. People said, "They're brushing down the couch, the bridegroom's coming to call – for his soup…"

Marie: How did your relationship develop in Terezín?

Věra: Our time together in Terezín brought us even closer together. By the time my parents left on a transport in 1943, my feelings for Valtr were so strong that I stayed behind with him. It was actually my mother who decided the matter when she said: "Your place is now by Valtr's side, we are your past, but Valtr is your future." When my people left I drew even closer to Valtr and realized that I could not leave him, then or ever. It was the most beautiful time of my life – sad, of course, and tragic – but our relationship was clear, and so refined. We knew we belonged to each other, it made us feel utterly secure, the knowledge that I had chosen him and that I was the one he had chosen.

Jiří Metzl
(b. 1929, perished).
Drawing.
Pencil, 210 × 185 mm.
Jewish Museum, Prague,
Inv. No. 129181.

Marie: Věra, I've often wondered what made you follow Valtr voluntarily to Auschwitz and in what way this decision influenced your future life. You could have stayed behind, couldn't you? [...] But perhaps if you hadn't gone, there would always have been something that would not have let you rest. You would have said to yourself: it might have turned out differently if I'd gone with him. You went to the limits with him. Is this perhaps why your life, though you've remained alone, is so untroubled?

Věra: I don't know. I didn't think about it like that at the time, I just did not want to be without Valtr, I was empty of all feelings without him, I was not myself... I just had to follow him. We had promised each other that I would come after him... And that it was Auschwitz I went to... If I had known where I was going – but I didn't know... Even life in Terezín was no longer possible for me, there was no other solution for me after all that. I am glad I went with him.

Marie: And after the war?

Věra: I ended up in Mauthausen, and we came home late, at the end of May. I went back to Solopysky – alone, but there I learned that my sister had had a breakdown in the concentration camp of Bergen-Belsen, so I went there to get her. We came back together and started looking for the others. I regularly went to Prague, searching for Valtr. I even started looking through the lists of the dead... One day, on the way back to Solopysky from Prague, my sister was silent and somehow not herself. The following day she said: "I opened one of your letters for the first and last time in my life. Don't go to Prague any more, don't search through the lists, here's your answer..."

Marie: How did you manage to come to terms with the knowledge that you had lost him forever?

Věra: That was very difficult, very difficult indeed. Valtr was no ordinary human being – and I was always comparing. After some time I tried to start a relationship so I wouldn't be alone, but it always broke down because it was not Valtr. Perhaps I idealized him with the passing years, perhaps everything would have been different if we had met again... I remember what a shock it was for me when I learned that friends of ours, who had married in Terezín as we had, separated after the war. I didn't believe it was possible for people who had gone through so much together to suddenly run away from it all... It is one of my nightmares to this day that the war is over and Valtr is alive somewhere – and he is not with me! And I say to myself: that's impossible, that could not have happened to us. And then I wake up and feel relieved that we did not fall apart like that ...

170

Josef Novák
(b. 1931, perished).
"Motifs from Terezín."
Pencil, 256 × 245 mm.
Jewish Museum, Prague,
Inv. No. 133502.

From
Valtr Eisinger's
letters
to Věra Sommerová

Brno, May 18, 1941

... but what separates me from you is not fate; it is unheard-of evil inflicted on us by the social system, a tremendous defeat for human freedom and pride. And that hurts enough to break your heart. That is a defeat from which we, the oppressed nations, are never supposed to recover. If it should really turn out that way, as proclaimed by the official view of this place in which we suffer, we two would never see each other again. But I am convinced that it will not turn out this way. I believe that we shall meet again, and meet as free and happy people.

Brno, January 7, 1942

... And since I have plucked one gloomy string, let me pluck another one, equally sad: at the end of this month another transport will leave Brno. We must take it as certain, though nothing is official as yet. But we are already doing the preparatory work. Irrespective of the fact that we from the Jewish community will probably be protected again – since it is we Jews who have to do all the hard work, both prior to the departure of the transport and afterwards, ourselves – despite that our mood is very dark indeed. Again the terrible memories of the previous transports are called to mind, the heart-rending scenes in the early morning dawn when people are interned in the barracks... If I did not know so many of the people personally, if I did not recognize our innocent children ...!

Brno, January 21, 1942

My Dearest Věra,

You did not expect this, and neither did I. But it has come. I will be included in the fourth Brno transport, which will assemble in the barracks on Sunday morning. It will probably leave Tuesday or Thursday, possibly on Wednesday of the following week.
   The die has been cast...
   I have calmly accepted the inexorable call

of our Jewish destiny, and it is my greatest wish that you remain calm, too. My parents already know about it; I phoned through to the Jewish community in Podivín. My darling Věra, you know what that means to them. Please fulfil my ardent wish, write to them often, at least once a week, and pray that they may survive. Write to them that you have definite news that everything in Terezín is all right, etc.
   I bless fate again that you are not with me, that you are spared all this. I am convinced that in the countryside, people's turn will not come so soon, and perhaps not at all.
   Apart from that I also firmly believe something else, so that I say goodbye to you in the firm conviction that we shall meet again, not in T[erezín], but as free people. And then, my beloved Věra, I shall realize the dream I so often dream ...!
   I shall always think of you, my thoughts of you will be my morning prayer when I get up, my evening prayer when I go to bed. My memories of you will be balm to whatever blows fate deals me.
   But my dearest Věra, should it happen that I do not return, I set you free of any promise you made me. I would only wish that the one to whom you give your hand should love you at least somewhat the way I love you....

Both sides of Valtr
Eisinger's postcard from
June 15, 1944 (pre-printed
thanks for a parcel).
Provided by the authors.

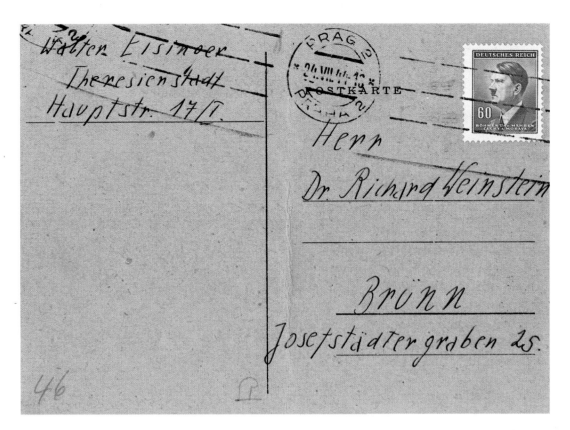

Theresienstadt, am 15. VI. 1944.

Liebster Ríša,

Ich bestätige dankend den Empfang Ihres (Deines) Paketes

vom 15. Juni 1944.

Innigsten Dank für das schöne Hochzeits-
geschenk. Dein   Walter Eisinger
                                            Unterschrift.

215

The Heart

In every heart, in a nameless corner
There's probably a tiny room
Where a man cherishes his "I"
Like a ring on his little finger.

A terrible burden I cherish there,
So many feelings without a name
And I cannot express them.
I am an echo in the wind.

My child, when he is born,
Eager to live, will be a man
May he never live through
What I have seen and suffered.

I do not know what name to give
To my small room with its small door,
Perhaps a bird will whisper a message
In my ear like an echo.

Perhaps my child will say:
"Dad, I know how you are."
My heart is so cruel to me
It will not let me dream,
But always says:
"My good man –
How would you put me into words?"

Today I said: the heart is a fire,
I have no strength to put it out.

– Academy (*Hanuš Hachenburg*)

Both sides of a postcard from June 26, 1944, in which Valtr Eisinger announces his marriage in Terezín to Věra Sommerová. Provided by the authors.

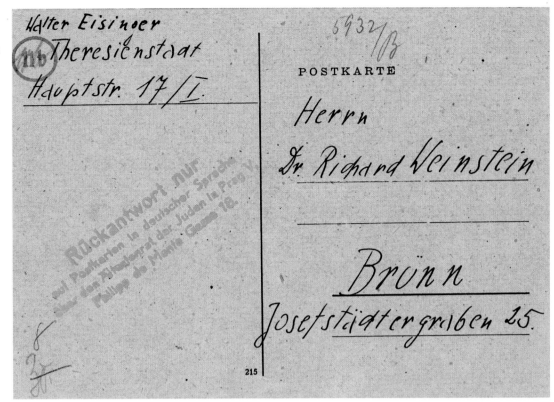

Walter Eisinger
Theresienstadt
Hauptstr. 17/I.

POSTKARTE

Herrn
Dr. Richard Weinstein

Brünn
Josefstädtergraben 25.

Lieber Riša!   26/VI.
Dein Paket innigst dankend erhalten. Mache mir immer größere Gewissensbisse, wie Du dazu kommst, solche Opfer für mich zu bringen. — Halte dich fest, ich habe geheiratet. Es tat uns sehr weh, daß Du nicht dabei warst. Wir wurden — selbstverständlich — zivil getraut. Bruno und Ernst fungierten als Trauzeugen.
Du fehlst mir sehr, sehr. Habe von Dir schon lange Wochen keine Karte erhalten. — Meine Schwester, mein Schwager und Lagy haben geschrieben. Auch Věrka hat von ihren Verwandten Nachricht erhalten. Blaß von Deinem und meinem Bruder weiß ich nichts. Ansonsten alles gesund und bester Mutz. Mit Ernst wieder die alten guten Freunde. — Věrka schickt Dir einen schönen Kuß. Ich grüße Dich und Deine Familie aufs innigste.
Dein Valter

Heroica

When the stormy wind whips up the ocean waters
And gulls seek refuge on the tossing mast
Oh then I never never feel unhappy
My soul of these wild terrors takes no heed.

When stormy waves break hard against the bulwarks,
And all take shelter in the hold below,
Wringing their hands in deep and dark despair
My soul amidst this tempest is at peace.

But when the sun's rays flow from azure skies
And gild the quiet waves and make them glitter
And all on board rush out and man the deck,
I find no joy in this tranquility.

For life is full of struggle and of wonder
And rallies when hard battle is at hand.
A man must always long to be a victor,
Prepared to win his fortune every day.

– Ha- (*Hanuš Hachenburg*)

The Poem "Heroica" is probably one of the first of Hachenburg's poetic attempts that have survived. It was written in response to Lermontov's poems. Hachenburg is said to have written it when he was still living in the Prague orphanage. He was twelve at the time.

Hanuš Hachenburg was born on July 12, 1929. He lived with his mother and probably never knew his father. On October 24, 1942, Hanuš was deported from the Prague orphanage to Terezín. In the beginning he lived in "Home Number Two," but Valtr Eisinger soon realized that this was an unusually talented boy and succeeded in having him transfered to "Number One." For a whole year Hanuš was one of the most frequent and admired contributors to the magazine *Vedem*.

Hanuš Hachenburg
(b. 1929, perished).
Title page for the puppet
play *Looking for a Ghost*
with his own illustration.
Pen, brush, aquarelle,
196 × 294 mm.
Memorial of Terezín,
Vedem – supplement after
p. 789.

VEDEM, Terezín 1942–1943

Leader

Yes, I take refuge in a leading article as the last possible experiment to justify myself in your eyes – the public. I don't write to achieve a reputation as a poet, but because I cannot express myself in any other way. I cannot express myself any other way because circumstances once taught me and compelled me to do so. It happened in the orphanage. I was a somewhat spoiled child of strange opinions and manners, raised in luxury and contemptuous of the poor beggarly riff-raff. When I came to the orphanage my reputation preceded me, and then accompanied me like an identification tag for the five years I was there. I had to confide in someone, so I confided in paper. Paper is silent, it can take anything. I could pour out my anger, I could weep, and I could rejoice. I know from experience that when a person has a sincere friend to whom he can air his complaints, he does not write poems, at least not poems about his own personality, or only very few. For me, poems are what friends are to other people. They are what I cannot tell anyone, because they would laugh at me. The incomprehensibility of my former poems was intentional. I wrote them so that not everyone would be able to understand them, penetrate them, and then laugh at me. I wrote them so they could only be fully understood by someone who was somewhat like me, or who had had similar experiences. I am not giving you a guide to understanding my poems. But I hope that after you have read these few lines and some of the little verses of mine that follow, I will have succeeded, not in becoming popular, but perhaps in coming closer to people of my age, something I have longed for over the last five years.

For Children

We are all children, little ones,
Playing with a colored ball.
We cry easily with ruddy cheeks
And then, with glowing faces
We look at a silvery world,
At green hillsides,
At life. We look ahead.

We are soft deer,
Complaining to crows
We think that we live
But merely accept blows.
We are all children,
Playing with the globe,
Water sprites
Pursing our lips
To receive our mother's milk,
                    peace,
                              life.
We are all people,
That is, we are matter.
The millwheel of time turns
Our feathers are drying, drying.
We scratch away in the night
Over our blouses
That take away our eyes
And in the day we are only in darkness.
We are all people
Gambling for the globe,
And the globe turns in blood
And turns and turns
And we reach out
For the small lights in the night
We children, children
Of a great revolution
We want to learn
So that from the earth we might
Freely drink
              Live
                    Triumph.

– Ha- (*Hanuš Hachenburg*)

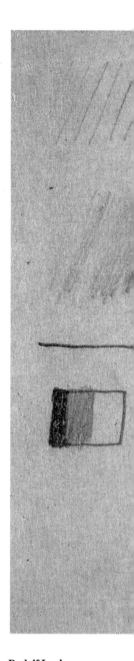

Zdeněk Ornest
Remembers

It was a special friendship – me and Hanuš. It actually began in the orphanage and then continued in the Home. Our friendship had its ups and downs, its crises. Hanuš was a little odd and so was I, and we often quarreled, but we had interesting discussions. Hanuš impressed me because he wrote poems. He was extremely well read and unusually knowledgable for his age. He was a pale, weak boy, and what I remember most vividly are his eyes. He was physically in very poor condition, impractical, always somewhere up in the clouds, his feet barely on the ground…

And then, in December, 1943, he was deported to the East. It was the only such case in our Home at the time, and thus it was that much greater a shock for me…

I learned later that Hanuš had ended up in the "family camp" of Auschwitz-Birkenau and that he had not come back.

VEDEM, Terezín 1942–1943

I, a tiny creature, beg the world for alms,
That it might not pound me down with its elephant feet,
That it might not burn me up with its fiery brand
Let me live till I'm too old to suckle the breast,
To fight like a man in this age-old struggle.

I want to live! I'm hungry. I thirsted after knowledge,
Fate offered it to me soft and smooth
Like a bag of candies with bitter filling
I, a sweet-toothed child, took and tasted
A candy, sweet at first, then an apple of knowledge.
The waves conspired against me, and fate was smooth
Laughing at me, laughing. From the clouds the snow burns.
The waves drive me, the waves devour me.
Time passing throws faded flowers on the rubbish heap,
And many I know used to live from them.

I suckle, I drink, and fate offers me its breast,
Though the milk it gives me is no longer sweet,
I and my thoughts are alone together now
We swallow more milk than we need, like smoke.

– Ha- (*Hanuš Hachenburg*)

Lenka Lindtová
(b. 1930, perished).
Collage, 190 × 145 mm.
Jewish Museum, Prague,
Inv. No. 121836.

My Country

I carry my country in my heart,
It is for me, and for me alone!
Woven from the beauty of fabric
It remains an eternal dream.

I kiss my land and caress it,
Passing much time in its presence.
This land is not on this earth
Yet it is within us everywhere.

It is in the heavens, in the stars above,
Wherever the bird nation lives.
I see it again in my soul today,
And my heart is heavy with tears.

One day I shall fly to the heights above,
Free from my body's encumbrance,
Free in expansiveness, free in distance,
And free with me, my country.

Today it is small. A handful of dreams
Encloses its distant horizons
And through the heavy dreams
Shimmer the furies of war.

One day I shall enter my country,
I shall rejoin my motherland,
There is my country! There is yours!
There is no "I" and no misery.

– Ha- (*Hanuš Hachenburg*)

Eva Kohnová
(b. 1932, perished).
Collage, 305 × 225 mm.
Jewish Museum, Prague,
Inv. No. 125721.

On December 18, 1943, **Hanuš Hachenburg** was deported to the "family camp" in Auschwitz-Birkenau, along with his mother. All trace of him vanished there. We asked for information about him at the Tracing Office for Missing Persons of the International Red Cross in Arolsen, Germany. From 1945 onwards, using surviving archives, this institution conducted research about prisoners from the Nazi prisons and concentration camps and assembled vast quantities of information. But concerning the tragic end of Hanuš's life there was only a single item: deported on December 18, 1943, from Terezín to Auschwitz. There is no further written information.

And so it was only through verbal reports that we learned that Hanuš had managed to survive for a time in the "family camp" and that he continued to write poems there. Some of his former Auschwitz fellow prisoners remembered his

182

poem "The Gong," which became so popular
that it was circulated among the prisoners. It
was based on a regular morning occurrence, the
gong that woke the prisoners. In their dreams,
they had returned to their homes, and it was the
gong that brought them back to the merciless
reality of the concentration camp, with its
hunger, filth, and the constant threat of death.
"The Gong" was the fourteen-year-old Hachenburg's literary farewell to life.

VEDEM, Terezín 1943

Faith
in Nothing

I am alone
I dreamt deceptive dreams
I am alone
In the distance, shelters collapse
I am alone
Black clouds of terror pass
I am alone
We are only wrecks on the sea.
I am alone
Flames pour over in waves
I am alone
And I fall over the foam
I am alone
I am only rags on bone,
I am alone
I have lost my strength, my breath.
I am alone
In the gardens roses grow,
I alone
Walk with you silently, close by.
Alone am I.
I can embrace the glow,
Because I am alone,
Of God's shining heaven.

I am alone.
Everything is born
In loneliness
That the world might drink its fill.
I am alone
In ashes left by flames
And I know:
There is nothing.

– Ha- (*Hanuš Hachenburg*)

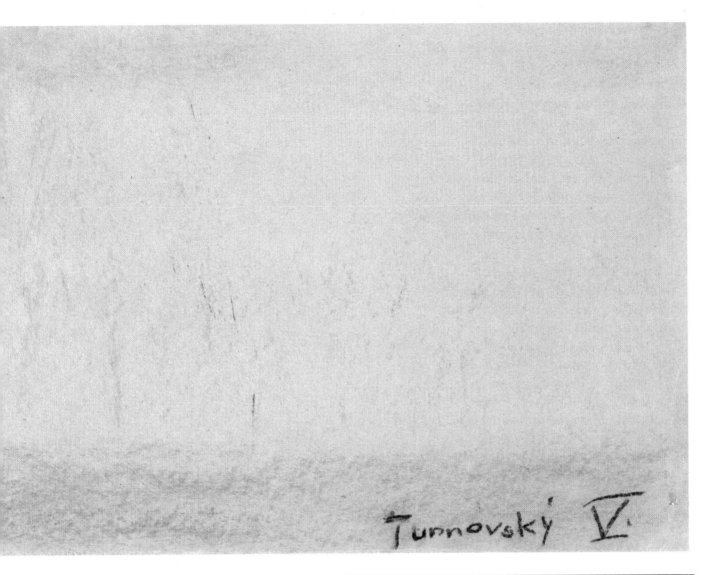

Hana Turnovská
(b. 1932, perished).
"Landscape."
Crayons, 250 × 175 mm.
Jewish Museum, Prague,
Inv. No. 121626.

Summer Noon

The sky is blue, lit by a glorious sun,
The sad treetops whisper, their branches spread like dreams,
Birds warble in many-colored splendor:
A summer's day.

A summer's day in chains, in bloody fetters,
A summer's day of hope, and light, and sun,
A black, black day lies polished like a boot
Black upon a pillow of green pine.

Dark, mighty gongs ring changes round my head,
I twist in radiance like a barrel organ
What noise is here. And what wheezing tumult.
How the air trembles. Leaves fall from trees.

What strong hand winds its sinews round and round me?
Another new emotion? And what of my will?

And then I saw a line rush through the air,
A surging mass of people, fallen heroes,
A mighty wind galloping by their side
Veiling the thousands in oblivion.

They are near me now: on horseback and on foot
They march, blood flowing from their wounds;
The sound of hoofbeats drowned out by the storm.
I find myself with three men, quite alone.

Three men holding their heads erect
Even in death, their faces lifted to the sky.
Thus they stood upon their chariot of war,
Rising on a mighty cloud of mist.

One of them turned and beckoned to me to come
And I stepped up onto his heavenly plough
The winds rose again, began to blow
We galloped madly into distant fields.

I took a closer look at those three figures
Now coursing swiftly through the stormy wind
And who did I see? Nelson the Admiral,
Ahasver, the third an unknown shadow.

How they talked! Holding their vigorous steeds
Close to the course, the two I recognized
Boasted in ringing words of victories
Till the black mists sighed, turned into clouds of ice.

And then I stepped out of the darkening shadow
To face the last of them. "Well, then," I asked,
"Why did you perish, or what have you achieved?"
The wind fell, the raging tempest ceased,

And far away, a scarlet band of light
Seeped through the crack where heaven meets the earth.
Cold pearls showered down upon us from above
I felt a cold breath touch my back, the god of night.

"I am no one, I am small, I have no name!"
Was that a voice or just the echo of the storm?
"I died for my ideals on the scaffold,
All my hopes drowned in a sea of blood."

Alice Sittigová
(b. 1930, perished).
Collage, 350 × 250 mm.
Jewish Museum, Prague,
Inv. No. 121766.

186

A summer's day enfolds this dream of night.

The greatest of all are those without a name,
The dying and the dying and the dead.
We follow in the traces of their blood
To paradise.

– Ha- (*Hanuš Hachenburg*)

"We Old Heroes, Warriors for the Young": A Manuscript Found on July 4, 1950

The war is now over, a war that has silenced millions of hearts, that has broken three quarters of our number. Millions have fallen, millions with a smile on their faces, beneath a tattered flag, a tin cross of courage. Millions of brave and tired hearts have stopped beating, hearts that had always beat honestly. But the crosses, the crosses will silence those millions of hearts. The crosses that dirty and besmirch their graves were forged by false and deceiving hands, hands that bathed in milk while they bathed the bodies and hearts of others in blood. Now the war is over, only a quarter of us are left. Of the others, crosses alone mark their memory. Only now do we see what crosses and banners mean. What of those rigid, silent crosses now? What of those blood-stained banners? Now, after the war, even to lament all this wickedness is already balm to our wounds. The sky is blue and the sun is shining, yet in the distance, far away, a small dark cloud has drawn up. This little cloud means war in the distance, a cloud that would overshadow the whole sky, that would destroy millions. This little cloud calls for utter destruction, calls for those who can hear it to destroy, to set the firmament ablaze. We, the old ones, are worn out, no longer of any use. It is up to you, and you alone, to make the sport of crosses unfashionable. You are the last bastion in the struggle. You must fight to bury all crosses deep in the earth. He who cannot do without crosses is a weakling. Let him stay at home.

But it is not your only task to fight without crosses. That is only one small step toward driving that cloud away. It is your task to rid the world of the tempest of war, to build a dam to hold back the old and evil world, a huge dam that cannot be swept away. You must form your ranks under one flag, the best, that will lead you forward to victory, and then plant that flag on the pinnacle of that dam! May your flag not be a mere rag. Let it be your shield, a shield of justice, truth, and love. You must not hide behind this shield. The shield must not weaken your conscience. Let the shield be only the symbol of your striving, striving toward the birth of a new life.

– *Hanuš Pollak*

These words that come to us, as it were, from the other side of the grave, were probably written in the late summer of 1944, just before the liquidation transports to Auschwitz, where Hanuš Pollak clearly perished. This is how the young author foresaw his fate and that of his comrades. But all his longing is fully directed to the future.

Edita Polláková
(b. 1932, perished).
Drawing, 240 × 230 mm.
Jewish Museum, Prague,
Inv. No. 129400.

189

Ruth Weissová
(b. 1931, perished).
"Seder."
Pastel, pencil,
305 × 205 mm.
Jewish Museum, Prague,
Inv. No. 129044.

**A list of the boys
from Home Number One in L 417,
drawn up in 1947
by Kurt Kotouč and Jiří Brady**

Bacon, Juda survived
Bauer, Jiří perished
Beamt, Hanuš perished
Beck, Hanuš perished
Benjamin, [?] perished
Bienenfeld, Zdeněk perished
Blum, Bedřich perished
Boskovic, Jan survived
Brady, Jiří survived
Brod, Toman survived
Bruml, Jiří perished
Bunzel, Adolf survived
Feuerstein, František perished
Fischer, Kurt perished
Fischl, Herbert perished
Fischl, Petr perished
Freund, Zdeněk perished
Frisch, Jiří perished
Gelb, Robert perished
Gelber, Petr perished
Ginz, Petr perished
Glasner, Kurt perished
Goldstein, Pavel perished
Gottlieb, Rudolf perished
Grünbaum, Jiří perished
Grünwald, [?] perished
Haas, Rudolf perished
Hachenburg, Hanuš perished
Heller, Hanuš perished
Herrmann, Jiří perished
Hoffmann, Bedřich perished
Immergut, Adolf perished
Kahn, Hanuš perished
Kalich, Hanuš perished
Kauders, Hanuš perished
Kaufmann, Beno perished
Kohn, Arnošt perished
Kominík, Hanuš perished
Kopelovič, Mendel survived
Kosta, Jiří perished

Kotouč, Kurt survived
Kraus, Hanuš perished
Kummermann, Pavel survived
Kurschner, Felix survived
Laub, Rudolf perished
Lax, Petr perished
Lebenhart, Jiří perished
Lichtenstein, [?] perished
Liebstein, Karel perished
Löwy, Leopold survived
Löwy, Wiki perished
Maier, Herbert perished
Marody, Leoš perished
Metzl, Jiří perished
Morgenstern, Emanuel perished
Mühlstein, Emanuel perished
Neumann, Miroslav survived
Ohrenstein (Ornest), Zdeněk survived
Pacovský, Ota perished
Picela, Norbert perished
Pick, Harry perished
Pick, Jiří perished
Pick, René perished
Pollak, Erik survived
Pollak, Hanuš perished
Pollak, Zdeněk perished
Popper, Ralph perished
Rosenberger, [?] perished
Roth, Walter perished
Sedláček, Otto perished
Segal, Kurt perished
Šindler, Otto perished
Stern, Harry perished
Stern, Karel perished
Sternschus, Hanuš perished
Tauber, Wiki perished
Taussig, Jiří perished
Taussig, Zdeněk survived
Teichner, Herman perished
Tenzer, Egon perished
Vielgut, Bedřich perished
Vohryzek, Jiří perished
Vohryzek, Zdeněk perished
Volk, Jan (Jiří) perished
Weil, Hanuš perished
Weinberger, Zdeněk perished
Weiner, Zdeněk perished
Weisskopf, [?] perished
Willheim, Laci perished
Zappner, Jiří perished
Žatečka, Jaroslav survived
Zinn, Erich perished

Epilogue

Terezín is a former fortress built under Emperor Josef II, not far from the confluence of the Labe and the Ohře rivers in Northern Bohemia. It was here, in 1941, that the Nazis established a ghetto for the Jewish population of Czechoslovakia and other European countries. From Terezín, prisoners were sent to slave labor camps and, more frequently, directly to the gas chambers of Auschwitz.

In the tragic struggle for survival the Nazi-imposed Terezín "self-administration" tried to help the imprisoned children. They were placed in buildings where the living conditions were better than in the many barracks inside the fortress or the other miserable lodgings where the grown-ups were kept. They were entrusted to pedagogues and had some medical care.

Title page, *Vedem*, double number 44–45, October 29, 1943.
Drawing by an **unknown artist**.
Pen, brush, ink, aquarelle, 202 × 300 mm.
Memorial of Terezín, *Vedem* p. 303.

Text in the drawing:
"*Vedem* destroys the old orders."

194

"I was one of these children," George Brady recalls. "And by pure luck I found myself among the boys who were led by Valtr Eisinger. In a small room overcrowded with three-tiered bunks, he created a new, fascinating world for us behind the ghetto walls. The boys developed talents they never dreamed they had, and it was there too that the illegal children's magazine on which this book is based was founded.

"About one hundred boys passed gradually through Eisinger's group, but only fifteen of them lived to see the liberation. One of them is Zdeněk Taussig, who rescued the magazine in Terezín and now lives in the United States. Taussig handed the magazine to me in Prague in 1945 and before I emigrated to Canada I passed it on to Kurt Kotouč, who was the chairman of our home's self-government under Eisinger in Terezín. Now the approximately 800 pages of the original magazine are in the Memorial of Terezín.

"The prose and poems of the boys who contributed to the magazine speak with such urgency and vitality that they cannot be left to collect dust in a museum. This is why I was particularly interested in a report from Czechoslovakia in early 1972 that the work was going to be published in book form. The editorship was assumed by Kurt Kotouč and Zdeněk Ornest, both of whom had taken part in the creation of the original magazine in Terezín. They were joined by Marie Rút Křížková, who wrote to me of her deep and strong feeling for this work. Here is her letter."

Prague, February 22, 1972

Dear Jirka,

Between the lines of your letter I sense a delicate question about my motives for taking on this task. Am I by any chance related to any of the authors of *Vedem*? Your question reminded me of the time ten years ago when I began to assemble Jiří Orten's literary estate and tried to convince the "competent authorities" that Orten's prose should be published. They answered me with a question: "Are you a relation of his?… Then you must be a Jewess… No?… Why are you doing it then?"

I was silent then and I shall remain silent now. I could invent some noble and persuasive motives, but the truth is simple: I don't know.

Once, when I was barely eighteen, I heard a call. I replied, "So be it," but I could only respond with my whole life. Let others judge the meaning of this encounter, and the worth of my response.

I will keep to the bare truth.

It was the poet Jiří Orten. On his twenty-second birthday, August 30, 1941, he had a fatal accident and died on the morning of September 1, shortly before the fascists made wearing of the Star of David "law." At the time, the little word "Jew" stood between us. It condemned him to annihilation and me to survival. It was a cruel and senseless destiny. It ordained that we could never meet, that we could be forever lost to each other. I longed to turn back the clock,

View of the battlements – the historical fortified walls around Terezín. Photograph by Vlasta Gronská, 1972.

Death mask of the poet **Jiří Orten** (1919–1941). Jewish Museum, Prague, Neg. No. 30037.

to nullify what divided us. But there was only pain and futility.

In time I came to another resolution: to cancel out what divided us by freely taking his lot upon my shoulders.

Jiří Orten's mother died on October 6, 1970. Shortly after that I wrote a timid, pleading letter to the Jewish Community in Prague. In the autumn of 1971, on Simchas Tora 5732, I was solemnly accepted into the Jewish Community in the Jerusalem Synagogue. I took the name of Rút. "For whither thou goest, I will go; and where thou lodgest, I will lodge; thy people shall be my people, and thy God shall be my God". (Ruth 1.16) That is my faith and my promise.*

And the book *We Are Children Just the Same* was to be my gift, an expression of my respect and gratitude to those who had accepted me with sincere kindness as one of them.

In 1967 Orten's brother, Zdeněk Ornest, let me read the raw manuscript of the Terezín magazine *Vedem* and asked me if I would take on the task of editing it. For three months, as I read it night after night, the question kept haunting me: by what law of justice did they perish and not I? In the end I gave it back. The work would have been insurmountable. Merely to decipher and transcribe the manuscript would have taken weeks and weeks. And perhaps I lacked the courage to identify with the fate of these children, who were destined to perish, and to go with them right to the door of the gas chamber.

I came back to the manuscript in 1971, when the time seemed ripe. I gave up my job as a grammar school teacher, left the town where I lived, and went to work and live with the children in the Jewish Religious Community in Prague.

So you see, Jirka, there can be no talk in my case of ownership or rights. In any case, without your and Zdeněk Taussig's efforts, who rescued and preserved the magazine, there could be no talk of our contribution at all. And finally: without your help, without the help of a number of friends at home and abroad, and without the close, daily cooperation of Kurt Kotouč and Zdeněk Ornest, this book would not have seen the light of day. Thus it is a collective labor in the truest sense of the word. We do not want the magazine *Vedem* to remain no more than an interesting document, a reminder of what has been and is now gone. We were led by a desire that the boys should come to life again in the pages of this text, in all their trusting youth and lust for life. At its deepest level, our book should bring our dead friends back to life and keep their memory alive in our hearts.
Yours,

Marie Rút

In the summer of 1972, I visited Czechoslovakia and once more read the texts that brought back to me the faces and voices of so many of my childhood friends whom fate had not permitted to survive. I assumed I was reading a manuscript ready for publication in book form. But three years later I met my friends again in Prague and learned that the book would not be published in Czechoslovakia.

(Prepared by K. K. on the basis of correspondence between Jiří Brady of Toronto and Marie Rút Křížková in Prague.)

Prague, March 1976

* A Catholic, Marie Rút Křížková is a member of the Society of Christians and Jews founded in Czechoslovakia in March, 1991. In January, 1977, she signed Charter 77, and in 1983 became one of its spokespersons. She worked as a forestry worker, later as a mail sorter on night shifts. She was not allowed to publish any of her own work until November 1989. At the moment she is preparing a critical edition of the works of Jiří Orten, to be published successively in nine volumes by the Český spisovatel Publishing House.

Review of the publication
*Small Lights in the Night**

Prague, January 26, 1973

I herewith return the manuscript of *Small Lights in the Night*, which I do not recommend for publication. An enormous amount of similar literature has been published in Czechoslovakia and to that material the present manuscript adds nothing new. Since 1967, Israeli propaganda has misused the persecution of the Jews during the Second World War to provide some sort of "moral justification" for Israeli aggression against the neighboring Arab nations. The publication of subject matter dealing with the persecution of the Jews must therefore be looked at with this point of view in mind. As long as the danger of war exists in the Middle East due to Israeli aggression and substantiated, moreover, by historical arguments, it is necessary to proceed with the utmost caution in the publication of such works. The cultural policy of a socialist state has clear-cut objectives and if the North Bohemian Publishing House has free capacity, authors must be chosen who reflect the intentions of this cultural policy in suitable ways. I am personally of the opinion that even in Prague there should be sufficient authors willing to contribute toward the realization of these objectives.

With comradely greetings,
Dr. Václav Král, DrSc.
Director, ČSI – ČSAV

(Czechoslovak Institute,
Czechoslovak Academy of Sciences)

Editor's Note

The complete collection of *Vedem* has been placed in the Memorial of Terezín. Together with illustrations it amounts to about 800 pages (the last eleven pages consist of a play, "Looking for Ghosts," by Hanuš Hachenburg). Up to page 190 it is typewritten, from page 191 onward (i.e., from No. 30 of July 9, 1943) it is handwritten, in both cases on sheets of A4 format. It "appeared" every week. The first number is dated December 18, 1942 and the last (No. 30, 1944) ends with page 789 and probably appeared on July 30, 1944.

We have arranged the texts according to subject matter, not date of publication. Subheadings like *Vedem*, Terezín 1943–1944, are followed by texts written within these years. Texts written later (conversations, memoires, etc.) appear in different typeface.

Each contribution from *Vedem* is followed by the symbol or pseudonym of its author. When we were able to decipher these, the real name of the author follows in parentheses. We know, for instance, that several boys signed themselves "Academy," but only rarely could we determine the original authorship.

We have omitted the last two verses from the introductory poem from which the original title of our book, *Are Ghetto Walls My Homeland?*, was taken

**I stand, and my soul proclaims:
I am a man of the world – Forward!**

Marie Rút Křížková

Title page, *Vedem* No. 19, April 23, 1943. (Headlines for the title pages were drawn by **Petr Ginz**.) Brush, aquarelle, typewriter, 200 × 298 mm. Memorial of Terezín, *Vedem* p. 119.

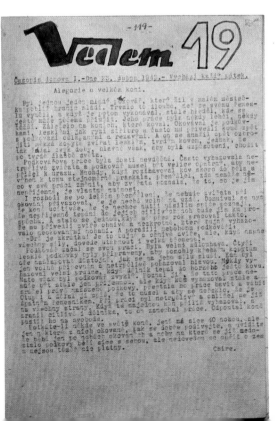

Acknowledgments

The publication and distribution of this book in English would not have been possible without the assistance and co-operation of many people. I would like to thank especially Václav Havel, President of the Czech Republic, for taking time from his full schedule to read the manuscript of the book and provide it with a wonderful Foreword. Thanks as well to Paul Wilson for editing and polishing the translation and assisting in other duties; to Adrienne Clarkson of the Canadian Broadcasting Corporation, and her producer Robert Sherrin, whose faith in the book took the concrete form of making a dramatized documentary on the subject and broadcasting it on "The Adrienne Clarkson Show" on CBC Television. And, for support in raising funds for the project, my thanks go to Nathan Leipciger of the Holocaust Remembrance Committee of Toronto.

Making a book of this nature, in cooperation with a publisher in the Czech Republic, has not been a simple matter, and I am grateful to the following people for help, financial support, and advice. They are: Mary Beck, Ernest Bloch, Doug, Paul, and David Brady, Bea Eisen, Abe Fish, Fedor Frastacky, Ruth Frish, David Geneen, Paul Goldstein, James Gutman, Susie Hickl-Szabo, Susana Justman, Anne Mandell, Joe Seidner, Isadore Sharp, Irwin Storfer, Joey and Toby Tannenbaum, Seymor Temkin. Without the help of all these people, and many others as well, this book might never have made it over the hurdles of international co-publication.

George Brady
Toronto 1994